OUR TOWN

OTHER TITLES IN THE GREENHAVEN PRESS
LITERARY COMPANION SERIES:

AMERICAN AUTHORS

Maya Angelou
Stephen Crane
Emily Dickinson
William Faulkner
F. Scott Fitzgerald
Robert Frost
Nathaniel Hawthorne
Ernest Hemingway
Herman Melville
Arthur Miller
Eugene O'Neill
Edgar Allan Poe
John Steinbeck
Mark Twain
Walt Whitman
Thornton Wilder

AMERICAN LITERATURE

The Adventures of
   Huckleberry Finn
The Adventures of Tom
   Sawyer
Black Boy
The Call of the Wild
The Catcher in the Rye
The Crucible
Death of a Salesman
Ethan Frome
Fahrenheit 451
A Farewell to Arms
The Glass Menagerie
The Grapes of Wrath
The Great Gatsby
Of Mice and Men
The Old Man and the Sea
One Flew Over the Cuckoo's
   Nest
The Pearl
The Scarlet Letter
A Separate Peace
To Kill a Mockingbird

THE GREENHAVEN PRESS
Literary Companion
TO AMERICAN LITERATURE

READINGS ON

OUR TOWN

Thomas Siebold, *Book Editor*

David L. Bender, *Publisher*
Bruno Leone, *Executive Editor*
Bonnie Szumski, *Series Editor*

Greenhaven Press, Inc., San Diego, CA

Every effort has been made to trace the owners of copyrighted material. The articles in this volume may have been edited for content, length, and/or reading level. The titles have been changed to enhance the editorial purpose. Those interested in locating the original source will find the complete citation on the first page of each article.

Library of Congress Cataloging-in-Publication Data

Readings on Our town / Thomas Siebold, book editor.
    p.   cm. — (The Greenhaven Press literary
companion to American literature)
    Includes bibliographical references and index.
    ISBN 0-7377-0189-7 (alk. paper). —
ISBN 0-7377-0188-9 (pbk. : alk. paper)
    1. Wilder, Thornton, 1897–1975. Our town. 2. City
and town life in literature. I. Siebold, Thomas. II. Series.
PS3545.I345O937   2000
812'.52—dc21   99-10188
                                                    CIP

Cover photo: Photofest. Thornton Wilder (center) portrays the Stage Manager in a 1938 production of *Our Town*.

Copyright © 2000 by Greenhaven Press, Inc.
PO Box 289009
San Diego, CA 92198-9009
Printed in the U.S.A.

"And as I view the work of my contemporaries I seem to feel that I am exceptional in one thing—I give (don't I?) the impression of having enormously enjoyed it."

Thornton Wilder, Preface to *Our Town*

CONTENTS

Chapter 1: The Format and Theatrical Principles of *Our Town*

Chapter 2: Themes and Characterization in *Our Town*

Chapter 3: Style and Criticism

Our Town, unlike most of the melodramatic and sentimental drama of Wilder's time, works to capture the inner reality of human experience.

FOREWORD

*"'Tis the good reader that
makes the good book."*

Ralph Waldo Emerson

The story's bare facts are simple: The captain, an old and scarred seafarer, walks with a peg leg made of whale ivory. He relentlessly drives his crew to hunt the world's oceans for the great white whale that crippled him. After a long search, the ship encounters the whale and a fierce battle ensues. Finally the captain drives his harpoon into the whale, but the harpoon line catches the captain about the neck and drags him to his death.

A simple story, a straightforward plot—yet, since the 1851 publication of Herman Melville's *Moby-Dick*, readers and critics have found many meanings in the struggle between Captain Ahab and the whale. To some, the novel is a cautionary tale that depicts how Ahab's obsession with revenge leads to his insanity and death. Others believe that the whale represents the unknowable secrets of the universe and that Ahab is a tragic hero who dares to challenge fate by attempting to discover this knowledge. Perhaps Melville intended Ahab as a criticism of Americans' tendency to become involved in well-intentioned but irrational causes. Or did Melville model Ahab after himself, letting his fictional character express his anger at what he perceived as a cruel and distant god?

Although literary critics disagree over the meaning of *Moby-Dick*, readers do not need to choose one particular interpretation in order to gain an understanding of Melville's novel. Instead, by examining various analyses, they can gain numerous insights into the issues that lie under the surface of the basic plot. Studying the writings of literary critics can also aid readers in making their own assessments of *Moby-Dick* and other literary works and in developing analytical thinking skills.

The Greenhaven Literary Companion Series was created with these goals in mind. Designed for young adults, this unique anthology series provides an engaging and comprehensive introduction to literary analysis and criticism. The essays included in the Literary Companion Series are chosen for their accessibility to a young adult audience and are expertly edited in consideration of both the reading and comprehension levels of this audience. In addition, each essay is introduced by a concise summation that presents the contributing writer's main themes and insights. Every anthology in the Literary Companion Series contains a varied selection of critical essays that cover a wide time span and express diverse views. Wherever possible, primary sources are represented through excerpts from authors' notebooks, letters, and journals and through contemporary criticism.

Each title in the Literary Companion Series pays careful consideration to the historical context of the particular author or literary work. In-depth biographies and detailed chronologies reveal important aspects of authors' lives and emphasize the historical events and social milieu that influenced their writings. To facilitate further research, every anthology includes primary and secondary source bibliographies of articles and/or books selected for their suitability for young adults. These engaging features make the Greenhaven Literary Companion series ideal for introducing students to literary analysis in the classroom or as a library resource for young adults researching the world's great authors and literature.

Exceptional in its focus on young adults, the Greenhaven Literary Companion Series strives to present literary criticism in a compelling and accessible format. Every title in the series is intended to spark readers' interest in leading American and world authors, to help them broaden their understanding of literature, and to encourage them to formulate their own analyses of the literary works that they read. It is the editors' hope that young adult readers will find these anthologies to be true companions in their study of literature.

INTRODUCTION

Since its New York debut in 1938, *Our Town* has fascinated more readers and audiences than any other play in the twentieth century. Despite its initial popularity, critics were not uniformly supportive of the drama. After all, Wilder had written anything but a conventional play, as his unconventional stage directions that introduce the action show:

No curtain, No scenery.

The audience arriving, sees an empty stage in half-light. Presently the Stage Manager, hat on and pipe in mouth, enters and begins placing a table and several chairs down stage left, and a table and chairs down stage right. As the house lights go down he has finished setting the stage and leaning against the right proscenium pillar watches the late arrivals in the audience.

Although *Our Town* genuinely moved audiences, some critics went on the offensive. The respected drama reviewer George Jean Nathan, called *Our Town* "a stunt." Others felt it was overly sentimental or lacked depth of character and meaning. Most, however, responded positively to the play's beauty, warmth, and sincere insights into the human condition. Ultimately, *Our Town* would enhance Wilder's reputation as a first-class American playwright.

Wilder once stated that he was not interested in creating make-believe on the stage; rather, he wanted to create an environment where audiences could sense the larger reality of who they are as they pass from birth to death. He does this by simultaneously portraying the commonplace events of everyday life and contrasting them with the universal. In the preface to *Three Plays* Wilder writes that he wanted to "find a value above all price for the smallest events of our daily life." In *Our Town* the audience enters the ordinary world of Grover's Corners and witnesses the activities of two small-town families, the Gibbses and Webbs. What they do is not unique; their actions, hopes, and fears are the same as millions of others. Through the quiet character of Emily, Wilder warns the audience that life goes by quickly and its beauty is too easily ignored. Although the playwright does not presume to provide an answer for the meaning of life, he leaves no doubt that life *is* meaningful.

Readings on Our Town is designed to help students gain a greater appreciation of Thornton Wilder's Pulitzer Prize–winning play. The carefully edited articles provide an overview of the play's themes, characterization, structure, philosophy, and impact on American theater. Each of the literary essays is readable, manageable in length, and focused on concepts suitable for a beginning exploration into the genre of literary criticism. In addition, this diverse overview of *Our Town* presents students with a wealth of material for writing reports, designing oral presentations, or enriching their understanding of drama as art.

THORNTON WILDER: A STUDY IN CONTRASTS

Edith J.R. Isaacs, editor of *Theatre Arts* magazine, remembers meeting Thornton Wilder in 1921 when Wilder was twenty-four years old. An aspiring playwright, he had just come from a postcollege year in Italy and France and was on his way to his first teaching job in New Jersey. On board the ship coming home he met theater reviewer Stark Young, who introduced him to Isaacs. After commenting on Wilder's having already "seen more of the world than many men ever see," Isaacs gives this picture of Wilder:

> It may have been something about the touch of many lands that gave him the double, but not at all divided, quality that is one of his distinguishing characteristics. Even in that first visit it was easy to see that although he was extremely serious, he was also very gay. Although very shy, he was unusually friendly; although he was surprisingly learned, he was never pedantic; he was as deliberate in his thinking as he was explosive in his speech, letting the words roll off his tongue one on top of the other but every one the right word aimed exactly at expressing the right idea. He was both temperate and enthusiastic, bold and unafraid but very modest, and above all he was one of the most amusing young men I had ever met.

This unassuming young man who went on to win three Pulitzer Prizes—unprecedentedly in two categories, fiction and drama—presented a series of contrasts in both his life and his work. An indifferent scholar, he was a voracious reader and an excellent teacher. He was a romantic at heart, but cast his works in classical form. His critical success was matched by popular acclaim; Bernard Grebanier, Brooklyn College professor emeritus of English, expressed the prevailing sense of surprise when he wrote: "Despite the three Pulitzer prizes awarded him Thornton Wilder may very well turn out to be one of the few enduring writers of our time."

AMOS AND ISABELLA WILDER

The contrasts in Thornton's life began with his parents, Amos and Isabella Wilder.

Amos Parker Wilder, son of a dentist who later founded a successful oilcloth manufacturing company, was raised in Augusta, Maine. He reported in the 1884 *Yale Class History* that during the after-school hours, "I was 'all over the place' . . . peddled things, carried water for elephants, worked in a grocery, and especially in a bookstore at odd hours." He was a bright and self-assured child, but when he entered the larger world of Yale University, his self-confidence suffered; "I was in terror of being dropped," he remembered later. Nonetheless, he was class orator in his first and second years, and Wilder biographer Linda Simon recounts some of his other academic and social successes:

> He was a member of Kappa Sigma Epsilon, Psi Upsilon, Skull and Bones; he sang in the class and university glee clubs, edited the *Courant* in his senior year, and acted as one of the class historians. His greatest disappointment—an embarrassment he was never to forget—came during his freshman year. He was selected for the staff of the *Record*, but was quickly dismissed for incompetency. "This was the severest humiliation I have ever known," he wrote later. In his small room on High Street he felt deeply dejected; but, characteristically, he summoned his strengths and rallied.

The humiliation may have spurred him to prove himself capable, for he later turned to the pen to make his living. After graduation, he taught school in Connecticut and Minnesota for a couple of years before taking a job as a reporter in Philadelphia. He then returned to New Haven for four years to earn a doctorate at Yale (his thesis was on municipal government) while editing the New Haven *Palladium.* He reveled in writing strongly opinionated editorials, one of which finally caused such controversy that he moved on to New York, where he worked for several papers. "Salaried journalism" did not have the job security he sought, though, so he bought a one-fourth interest in a Milwaukee, Wisconsin, newspaper, the *State Journal,* and became the paper's editor. Always one to keep busy, he also began giving a series of lectures on city government, sponsored by the University of Wisconsin.

In 1894 Amos married Isabella Thornton Niven, daughter of a Presbyterian minister from Dobbs Ferry, New York. The Wilders settled in Madison, Wisconsin, where their first son, Amos Niven, was born in 1895.

Isabella "was unlike her husband in temperament," notes Linda Simon:

> While Amos was outgoing, forceful, a fiery speaker, his wife was quiet and reserved. Though she had not been highly educated, she was artistic and refined. At Sunday school in her father's church, the teacher had found her "brilliant and highly cultivated." She had had aspirations of attending college or becoming a teacher, but her father, the Reverend Thornton MacNess Niven, had definite restrictions for the education of his daughter.... Amos, too, showed a skepticism of Isabella's artistic inclinations. He was ever the patriarch and, for his wife and some of his children, a formidable force to confront.

Deterred from achieving her own ambitions (she had wanted to become a physician, but her father forbade it even after she had been accepted by Barnard College), Isabella Wilder did not abandon her aesthetic interests. Despite having four children in five years, Simon notes, "Neighbors would often see her taking her children on afternoon outings: her oldest son, Amos, was barely walking, steadying himself by holding on to the baby carriage with the three younger children inside, and Isabella herself would be pushing the carriage as she read a book of poetry."

THE MISSING TWIN

Those four children had nearly been five: On April 17, 1897, Isabella Wilder bore identical twins, but one son lived only a few hours. The surviving twin was named Thornton Niven, for Isabella's father. Born prematurely and weak, he had to be coddled for weeks to insure his survival. Perhaps this less-than-hale-and-hearty start predisposed his father to think of him as unable to care for himself; Amos Wilder more than once mourned that this "poor boy" would always be a burden.

Surviving his twin affected Thornton throughout his life. When he was twenty, he wrote his father, "I suppose that everyone feels that his nature cries out hourly for it knows not what, but I like to believe that mine raises an exceedingly great voice because I am a twin, and because by his death an outlet for my affection was closed." In later years, his older brother, Amos, wrote:

> Though Thornton and I were not twins, I have always felt that there was some sort of occult affinity in my makeup for his fabulations, like the telepathic understanding between Manuel and Esteban in *The Bridge of San Luis Rey*. . . . As himself a twin who lost a brother at birth, he was predisposed

to fascination with this relationship. Indeed one could hazard that he was haunted all his life by this missing alter ego. Thus he plays with the afterlife of this twin in the dual *persona* suggested by the title of his last novel, *Theophilus North,* "North," of course, representing an anagram for Thornton. In this was he was able to tease both himself and the reader as to the borderlands between autobiography and fable.

Observers also labeled as "his missing twin" Thornton's sister Isabel, who in later years handled his business and personal affairs and served as his intermediary with the public when he disappeared to write. These characterizations point up the closeness the children maintained throughout their lives, nurtured in part by their father's insistence that they write thoughtful letters to one another during their many separations.

Those first few years, though, brought few separations. From spring to fall the family (which now included Charlotte Elizabeth, born August 28, 1898, and Isabel, born January 13, 1900) lived in a rustic cottage on Lake Mendota, four miles from Madison. Thornton, now called Todger, was no longer frail, and "all the Wilders were lively; indolence was as alien as luxury," writes Thornton biographer Gilbert A. Harrison.

"Their intellectual growth was overseen by both parents," Simon notes, "with each contributing something in accordance with his or her personality. Amos preferred Scott, Dickens, and Shakespeare; Isabella, Yeats and Maeterlinck. Amos was concerned with imparting moral lessons; Isabella, a sense of beauty."

A Larger Arena

By the turn of the century, the outspoken Amos Parker Wilder, who now held a controlling interest in the *State Journal,* had become an important force in state politics. This had not led to financial security, though; a ratings war between newspapers and Wilder's crusade against corruption and alcohol (he refused to run liquor ads) cut sharply into the Wilders' income, making it ever harder to support his growing family. Yet beyond financial considerations, it was a desire to find a larger stage for his talents and a larger audience for his strong views that led Amos Wilder to seek a political appointment. A friend from Yale, William Howard Taft (who would later be elected president), was the secretary of war in President Theodore Roosevelt's cabinet. After

Amos was passed over for his first choice, as U.S. minister to Uruguay-Paraguay, he called on Taft to support his appointment as consul general at Hong Kong. He was confirmed in the post on March 7, 1906, and on May 7 the family landed in Hong Kong.

Thornton was enrolled in a strict, German-language school in Hong Kong. He remembered being carried about in a sedan chair and coming home for lunch with Wong, the "number one boy." But Isabella was unhappy in the colony, and on October 30 the rest of the Wilder clan left Amos behind and returned to the United States, settling in Berkeley, California. Here Thornton—with his mother's help—found the theater. His sister Isabel recalled Berkeley in her 1977 foreword to Thornton's play *The Alcestiad:*

> The magnificent Greek theater built into the hillside of a eucalyptus grove was a new and lively part of the life of the university and the town. Several times a year the Classics Department mounted productions of plays by Sophocles, Aeschylus, and Euripides. Our mother joined the volunteer workers in the costume shop and stenciled furlongs of borders in the Greek key or laurel leaf patterns on gorgeously colored togas. She made a little blue one with shells around the hem for Thornton—and a green one for brother Amos—and sent them off to apply for roles as members of the Athenean mob. Thus Thornton discovered "total" theater and the Golden Age of Antiquity. His experience until then had been a performance of *As You Like It* seen from the top gallery of a Milwaukee theater.
>
> By now Thornton was ten; black-haired, blue-eyed, acquisitive and radiant. Even before this he had claimed his share of a writer's allotment of the twenty-six letters of the alphabet and had begun to tame them into a vocabulary that would allow him—in good time—to speak in his own way. He went to bed early and got up early to write, and the full range of his enlarging vocabulary was turned to inventing dialogue. He draped us and the neighbors' children in yards of begged or borrowed cheesecloth and coaxed us into declaiming his grandiloquent speeches.

In 1909, after Amos took the post of consul general in Shanghai, he made two trips to California to be with his family. (A third daughter, Janet, was born in 1910.) He was nearly a stranger to his children. When he returned to Shanghai, his frequent letters exhorted his offspring to follow his own stern precepts. He frowned upon the Greek theater ("As for Greek plays, you know Papa has only a limited admiration for 'art.' . . . *Character* is the thing in life to strive for"), and instructed the children to read aloud to one another *Pilgrim's Progress, The Vicar of Wakefield,* and *The Boy's Life of John Wesley.*

Although the family enjoyed Berkeley, money was tight. Consuls general were instructed to help U.S. firms establish overseas business. The positions paid a modest salary and required a fair amount of entertaining; it was assumed that the companies they helped would be generous in helping them cover their expenses. Amos Wilder, ever sternly righteous, would never accept such remuneration. (He also refused to help companies that sold alcohol, even when instructed to do so by the State Department; he offered instead his resignation, which was not accepted.) The money Amos sent to Berkeley ($1,500 of his $8,000 salary) did not go far to support his wife and five children, and after the birth of Janet, the strain led most of the family (the younger Amos remained in California) to reunite in China once again.

Charlotte and Thornton were sent to the China Inland Mission Boys and Girls School at Chefoo, in Shantung Province. They were there, 450 miles north of Shanghai, when Sun-Yat Sen led a revolution in central China and was proclaimed president of the new republic. The turmoil does not seem to have affected their schooling, although Thornton wrote to his mother that the revolutionary army had offered the school's servants twice their salary to enlist. "Result: boys work; result: Wilder washes dishes and cleans carrots, serves table and carries water for other people (boys) to wash in (not himself! Oh no!)."

Discipline at the school was strict and the academic requirements were tough, especially since his schooling in Berkeley had not prepared him with the competence that was expected in Greek, Latin, algebra, and geometry. He and Charlotte were allowed a few minutes together once a week. Gilbert Harrison reports that "uniformed in white pith helmets and white suits with knee-length pants, the boys were marched on Sundays through hot, dusty streets to attend Church of England services, seeing on all sides goiters, tumors, abscesses, stumps of lepers' arms and legs, the blind, the skeletal Chinese children. It was Thornton's first sight of omnipresent misery—untended, ignored, endured." That recognition of the endurance of the human race would form the basis of some of his most powerful works.

Once again, Mrs. Wilder was unhappy living with her husband in China; this time she took the two younger daughters, Isabel and Janet, to stay with her sister in Florence, Italy. Charlotte and Thornton stayed at Chefoo, their brother Amos was still in Berkeley, and their father was in Shanghai.

Thornton had persuaded the school authorities to let him substitute long-distance running for the required group sports of soccer and cricket. His father deplored his failure to be a sportsman—not realizing until some years later that his second son was severely nearsighted—but Thornton exulted in the long stretches of time alone: He knew that writers needed such time, and he used his running time for thinking.

Students were required to write their parents every Sunday, so Thornton had to write both to Shanghai and to Florence. His letters to his father rarely had trouble conforming to the school's standards (they were read by a teacher before they were sent), but his fanciful letters to his mother occasionally elicited the comment, "Too fantastic!"

A year later, Mrs. Wilder, Isabel, and Janet returned to the United States, while Thornton, Charlotte, and Mr. Wilder sailed for California from China. (Mr. Wilder had contracted a debilitating tropical disease, Asian sprue, that left him listless and unhappy. He had resigned his post, and would never regain the vigorous health he had enjoyed before.) Thornton joined Amos at the Thacher School in the Ojai valley in California, a school that normally attracted affluent students. The headmaster, Sherman Thacher, was another Yale buddy of Thornton's father's, and with his help the boys were able to get an education they could not otherwise easily afford. In *Thornton Wilder: An Intimate Portrait*, Richard Goldstone notes that Amos warned his old friend about his younger son:

> He had "nerves," was "silent, sensitive," and slept badly; he could swim, but beyond that had no interest in sports; his interests, rather, were directed toward "music, art, drama and literature"; he was "not a good mixer," but was sensitive and self-conscious, though "radiantly happy when with those who like and understand him." Amos added, in relaying these unfortunate characteristics to Headmaster Thacher, that "he may develope 'moods'."

It was about this time that their father demanded a pledge of temperance from Thornton and Charlotte; he made them sign a promise never to drink alcohol. In Thornton's case, that promise did not take; by his college years, he was regularly enjoying social drinking. (Years later, Richard Goldstone asked him, "One of your most celebrated colleagues said recently that all a writer really needs is a place to work, tobacco, some food, and good whisky. Could you explain to the non-drinkers among us how liquor helps things along?" Wilder replied, "My springboard has always been long walks. I drink a great deal, but I do not associate it with writing.")

In his foreword to *The Angel That Troubled the Waters and Other Plays,* Thornton remembered himself at sixteen:

> It is a discouraging business to be an author at sixteen years of age. Such an author is all aspiration and no fulfillment. He is drunk on an imaginary kinship with the writers he most admires, and yet his poor overblotted notebooks show nothing to prove to others, or to himself, that the claim is justified. The shortest walk in the country is sufficient to start in his mind the theme, the plan, and the title, especially the title, of a long book; and the shortest hour when he has returned to his desk is sufficient to deflate his ambition. . . .
>
> Authors of fifteen and sixteen years of age spend their time drawing up title pages and adjusting the tables of contents of works they have neither the perseverance nor the ability to execute. They compass easily all the parts of a book that are inessential. They compose dignified prefaces, discover happy quotations from the Latin and French, and turn graceful dedications.

That short attention span might have hampered a lesser writer, but Thornton kept writing a series of "three-minute plays for three persons." He went on to compose at least forty of these short works, finding in them "a literary form that satisfied my passion for compression" and avoided "the needless repetition, the complacency in most writing."

COLLEGE

After a year at Thacher, Thornton transferred to Berkeley High School, which Charlotte was attending, for two years, planning to attend his father's alma mater, Yale, when he graduated. But Amos Wilder feared Yale was too worldly for his spiritually inadequate son. Instead he enrolled Thornton in Ohio's Oberlin College, an evangelical college founded by two Congregational ministers, which Thornton's brother also attended. After two years, his brother was allowed to transfer to Yale, and Thornton wrote a friend that "I have [my father's] promise in writing for one year only." In the end, he spent two years at Oberlin, transferring to Yale under protest.

Although Amos had hoped Oberlin would mold his son into his own image, the Ohio campus held other interests for

Thornton. Among its many appeals, the school offered an excellent music department, an outlet for his passion for theater, and the "salons" of Mrs. Martin, the wife of one of the professors. Martin invited a circle of students to meet on Sunday afternoons. These salons were, writes Richard Goldstone, "of considerable importance to the young man's development of poise and self-assurance; there he could talk about theater, about new writers—George Moore was one of his enthusiasms—and he was respectfully listened to." He joined the editorial board of the *Literary Magazine* and was made archivist of the CYMOC club, a group of students that met monthly for intellectual discourse. (The members swore not to reveal what the initials CYMOC stood for.)

Besides the respect of his peers, Thornton was encouraged by Professor Charles H.A. Wager, the chairman of the English Department. Wager, whom Wilder described as "the greatest class lecturer I have ever heard," invited the young author home, "and encouraged him to read aloud the stories and plays which, a year or so before, he could show only to his mother," according to Goldstone.

So by the time Amos decided to transfer his younger son to Yale in New Haven (where the family was now established), Thornton was "completely devoted to Oberlin and deeply resented my father's moving me to the East." His father insisted, for several reasons: to bring the family together, to save money, and to earn a Yale diploma, which would be most valuable in finding a job in teaching, the profession he had decided on for Thornton.

During the summers, Amos required his sons to work at physical labor; he usually found a farm where they would be required to do chores in return for a small wage. Thornton also had one other break in his college career, from September 18 to December 31, 1918, when he joined the Coast Artillery Corps. He had long wanted to serve in the war being fought in Europe, World War I, but his nearsightedness had made him ineligible until just before the war ended. He resumed his studies in January 1919 and received his diploma in June 1920, listing his profession in the yearbook as journalist.

Not Exactly the Grand Tour

Thornton wanted to make his living as a writer; Amos thought that absurd. Richard Goldstone describes the father's worries:

Now fifty-six years old, his earning potential limited by age and dwindling opportunities, Amos, the head of a household consisting of four females and an elder son about to enter the ministry, saw in Thornton the only bulwark—and an insubstantial one at that—against poverty and disgrace should he, Amos, be stricken and incapacitated. Not for a moment did Amos entertain the thought that Thornton could, through writing, maintain even himself ("Carving olive pits!" "Carving olive pits!"). Viewing his second son as basically ineffectual, somewhat indolent, and not overly intelligent, Amos reached the conclusion that Thornton could eke out a living in the only way open to failures and incompetents: as a schoolmaster. Having arrived at that decision through his own inexorable logic, Amos communicated it to Thornton who, faced with the vision of his mother and sisters facing starvation, bowed to Necessity and accepted his Lot.

But first there would be a brief respite. Thornton would be allowed to spend a year as a resident visitor at the American Academy in Rome. He could learn Italian and brush up on his Latin—both useful for a teacher—while performing some healthy physical labor swinging a pickax at the school's archaeological digs. Why Italy? His mother had discovered that the exchange rate for dollars was at that time very favorable. After due consideration, Gilbert Harrison reports, Amos told his son:

> My dear boy, . . . I am going to give you $900, in installments. If the money situation over there is as your mother says it is, that will sustain you very well for a year. . . . So make the most of your advantages in Rome. When you return, I hope you will be prepared to teach Latin in some school somewhere, and as far as money is concerned, let me not hear another word out of you for the rest of our lives.

Although the more immediate product of Thornton's Italian journey was his first novel, *The Cabala*, part of the influence of this year abroad later found its way into Wilder's *Our Town*. In a preface for that play, he wrote:

> For a while in Rome I lived among archeologists, and ever since I find myself occasionally looking at the things about me as an archeologist will look at them a thousand years hence. Rockefeller Center will be reconstructed in imagination from the ruins of its foundations. How high was it? A thesis will be written on the bronze plates found in New York's detritus heaps—"Tradesmen's Entrance," "Night Bell."

> In Rome I was led through a study of the plumbing on the Palatine Hill. A friend of mine could ascribe a date, "within ten years," to every fragment of cement made in the Roman Republic and early Empire.

An archeologist's eyes combine the view of the telescope with the view of the microscope. He reconstructs the very distant with the help of the very small.

It was something of this method that I brought to a New Hampshire village.

LEARNING FRENCH

At the end of eight months, money running short, Thornton prepared to leave Italy. He had been hinting to his father that it would be a good idea for him to go to Paris (which was becoming a mecca to expatriate Americans, especially expatriate American writers), "to learn French." As one of the two positions Amos was contemplating for his son was as a teacher of French, he agreed to finance a few weeks in France but warned Thornton to return promptly, ready to teach the language at Lawrenceville, a New Jersey prep school. Lawrenceville agreed to hire Thornton for $1,500 per year on the recommendations of his Yale professors, and Thornton wrote to his mother (then in England): "Well, well, I am as excited as a decapitated goose." He enjoyed Paris, but returned early to New York to take French lessons at the Berlitz School.

MADE TO BE A TEACHER

Unexpectedly, Thornton enjoyed his new job, which included housemaster duties for the thirty-two boys who lived at Davis House. Nights after ten, weekends, and vacations were devoted to writing; the rest of his hours were devoted to his students. Gilbert Harrison writes that he was a popular teacher:

> The boys were entertained by his rapid walk and talk and grateful for his cheerful tolerance of their nonsense. He was *different.* "Mr. Wilder seemed to find us endlessly intriguing and disturbing," one of the boys, Marshall Sprague, recalled, "though we knew that his interest was that of a spectator at the zoo watching the monkeys, charming and repulsive by turns, happy to be noticed, especially when he erupted like a volcano at some misconduct of ours and threw blackboard erasers and chalk at us." They retaliated by dropping a trunk down the stairs from the third floor, so that it would knock the door off his room and end up inside. . . .
>
> He tried without conspicuous results to introduce French into everyday conversation. For the enlightenment of one lad who was having trouble with irregular verbs, in this instance the present tense of venir, he leapt over the back of a couch, flapping his arms and shouting "On wings of gauze they come!

they come! ILS VIENNENT!" . . . First-year boys were directed in scenes from a popular Broadway show, *Nelly Kelley,* taught to sing "Don't Send Me Roses When It's Shoes That I Need" and how to form a chorus line. Halfway through the study period, Mr. Wilder visited all rooms to observe work habits, decisively solving such problems as a snake crawling between sheets. At bed-check, he rushed to a window and shouted, "No, madam! You can't come in. This is a boy's room!" Yes, Mr. Wilder was *different.*

Thornton supplemented his salary with other small jobs: preparing a publisher's catalog and tutoring during the school year, more tutoring during summer breaks, and finally publication of a portion of the book he was working on, then called *Memoirs,* in a small New Orleans magazine, *Double Dealer.* He finally had enough money to send some to his family and offer, "Tell me when you need more."

THE PARENTAL INFLUENCE

Amos Wilder, who would die in 1935, no longer controlled his son's life. While biographers and critics uniformly agree that Isabella Wilder nurtured, supported, and encouraged her son's gifts, they disagree on the influence of Thornton's father.

At least one biographer, Richard Goldstone, believes Amos Wilder's influence on his second son was harmful. He notes that Isabella was unlike most American women, who stayed with their husbands in diplomatic postings and sent the children to boarding school:

> There is no avoiding what is more than a possibility that, in 1906, she effected the separation of her children from her husband because she had already observed that his influence was unwholesome and psychologically damaging. Not only did Amos's stern Calvinism hang like a cloud over the young children, but he imposed on them his iron will, his lofty standards of conduct, achievement, and principle, and his sense of himself—law-giver and dispenser of absolute justice. . . .

> Maintaining a fatherless household [in Berkeley] was to be a struggle—financial and physical—for Isabella. . . . But whatever the physical handicaps she encountered in making do with the meager allowance remitted by her husband, Isabella was enabled to remedy—if remedy she could—the psychologically crippling influence that her husband exerted upon their children.

Those who feel Amos was a hindrance rather than a brace to his talented son find support in such outbursts as Thornton's defense of himself and his oldest sister in this letter to his father, written when he was twenty-one:

Sometimes I get so annoyed by your desperation over a chance cigarette or a frivolous word that I have a good mind to give you a real jolt, such jolts as other fathers get from their sons, the real griefs of Old Eli [Yale]. I am too good for you, that's all, and you make a luxury of martyrdom to yourself out of my slightest defection. Likewise Charlotte's friends consider her an amazing, rare personality, such as New England is only able to cast up once in an age, but you wear us all out with your instigations to Napoleonship and fame [and] look upon the first YMCA secretary or Settlement House directress as more interesting than Charlotte. Do try to console and comfort your declining years with the incredible news that you have produced at least two children that are the amazement and delight and amused despair of their circles (the more finely grained the spectator the greater the appreciation). Let others produce obscure devoted women and faithful Assistant Pastors; you have fathered two wild fowl flying in the storm of the 20th century.

Thornton's brother offers a different perspective on biographers' speculations in *Thornton Wilder and His Public:*

It is inevitable that I should give special attention to the role of our father in my brother's development. . . . This parent of Maine background had certain of the robust and granitic traits and that "interfering spirit of righteousness" associated with the Calvinist heritage, a type widely derided today. My brother had his troubles with him. . . . But the paradox in this case was that this same overshadowing father was also the one who imbued my brother with his deepest insights into American grass-roots values and their hidden operations.

Although Thornton thought of his father as "a sort of Don Quixote" without any sense of the aesthetic, writes Gilbert Harrison,

Still, Thornton took from him a desire to shape and improve lives, a facility with language, a histrionic virtuousity, moral energy, nostalgia for small towns and respect for anonymous multitudes. . . .

However hard-pressed, he had always found the money a child needed. He had sent his son to farms not as punishment but to provide lessons in the value of the dollar and in health building. His strictures were not motivated by selfish concerns, certainly not by dislike. Whatever the frustrations of his married life, he held that "the drama of the home is a great mystery," a mystery Thornton would celebrate in his plays, and that nowhere else do all manner of men "grow tender and have longings to be good: hugging their children and walking about in the dark hours safeguarding their dependents." Moreover, Papa's conviction that literature would not pay was commonplace for his generation.

ROMAN MEMOIRS

At the end of the spring 1924 term, Thornton requested a two-year leave of absence from Lawrenceville, intending to finish his *Memoirs* and try to find a publisher. He spent that summer at the MacDowell Colony in Peterborough, New Hampshire, the first of several stays at the prestigious artists colony, where he was encouraged by the benefactor of the colony, Mrs. Edward Mac-Dowell, and managed to finish five of the portraits for *Memoirs.* At the end of that year, he submitted part of the manuscript to New York publishers Albert and Charles Boni. The Bonis were mildly encouraging and Wilder completed more sections; they finally offered him a contract in November 1925. By then Wilder had returned to school, attending Princeton to earn a master of arts degree in Romance languages. If the book—now called *The Cabala*—did not sell well, he counted on the M.A. to help him find better-paying work.

The book appeared in April 1926, and was hailed by the *New York Times* as "the debut of a new American stylist" and a "magnificent literary event." Other critics agreed, and sales were respectable. But when Thornton discovered that his contract said that no payment was due him until February 15, 1927, he realized he could not live on his earnings as an author just yet. He accepted a job as chaperone to Europe for a young man; he could travel and be paid for it, earning enough to last until Christmas. However, the young man, twenty-year-old Andy Townson, proved an uncongenial companion; by the time he left for home at the beginning of December 1926, Thornton was impatient to get back to work on his next book, *The Bridge of San Luis Rey.* He wrote his publisher and asked for $150 against his royalties so he could resume work on the book in Europe, now that he no longer had the Townson subsidy to cover his living expenses. He considered rooming with Ernest Hemingway to save money, but "his wife is about to divorce him and his new wife is about to arrive from America; so I think I better not try." He wrote, went to the Riviera for Christmas, dropped in on Sylvia Beach at her famous Paris bookstore Shakespeare and Company, and wrote his mother that he was homesick. At the end of January 1927 he sailed for home.

THE BRIDGE OF SAN LUIS REY

Occasional tutoring jobs to meet expenses continued to eat away at his writing time; when Lawrenceville invited him to return as master of Davis House, he agreed to come for one school year, 1927–1928. Perhaps the anticipation of a secure position helped; within two weeks of accepting the position, he finally finished the manuscript he had been working on, *The Bridge of San Luis Rey*. Ironically, when the book came out that fall, Thornton was recuperating from surgery for appendicitis and anxious to return to Lawrenceville; "otherwise, what will become of my SALARY."

The book was a smash hit. By December, it had earned him $20,000 in royalties—quite a sum for a man who was eager to return to a $4,000-a-year position as a school-teacher. The excitement—especially after the book was awarded the 1928 Pulitzer Prize for fiction—made teaching school difficult. But it did bring a measure of celebrity that had him hobnobbing with the famous: Gene Tunney, world heavyweight boxing champion, invited him to dinner (the two men, who got on well, would later go on a walking tour in Europe together). Broadway producer Jed Harris asked for the right of first refusal on Thornton's next play. And Scott and Zelda Fitzgerald invited him to spend a weekend with them at the house they had rented in Delaware.

Success

Thornton could do what he wanted now, without worrying overmuch about money. His mother had long wanted the family to have a house of their own; he purchased property in Hamden, Connecticut, in March 1929 and spent a substantial part of his new earnings on "The House *The Bridge* Built." With Thornton's help, his father, who was physically ailing, retired from working and spent much of the next few years in sanitoriums or on health farms. Besides supporting his parents, he also provided for Isabel (and, after the mid-1930s, for Charlotte); only Amos and Janet—the oldest and youngest siblings—were making their own way. Isabel began to take over the day-to-day work Thornton's celebrity necessitated; she dealt with his mail, acted as literary agent, served as hostess, dealt with the myriad details that did not interest Thornton. He never married, and this convenient arrangement continued until he died. Isabel often traveled with Thornton; besides running interference in practical matters, she was a congenial sounding board for his new ideas.

He was working on *The Woman of Andros* when the stock market collapsed at the end of October 1929, marking what would become known as the Great Depression. When the book was finally published, it did not seem appropriate or "socially relevant" during a period of widespread hardship; critics were especially hard on its foreign setting, and a vitriolic attack by proletarian writer Michael Gold in the *New Republic*, entitled "Wilder: Prophet of the Genteel Christ," lambasted him for not having written a novel about the working class. His next book, *Heaven's My Destination*, was a sympathetic and funny picture of middle America.

Chicago

Thornton still loved teaching, and had happily accepted a position at the University of Chicago for the appealing sum of $666.66 per month. He later said that his years in Chicago, 1930–1936, were the happiest of his life. He became a member of a group of men and women who were bright without being intellectual, fun loving and informal. The longtime loner ecstatically told his friend Alexander Woollcott, the *New Yorker*'s theater critic, "They love me humanly and I love them inhumanly."

Despite his new affluence, Wilder did not spend money easily on himself. "Things don't speak to me," he noted with dismay when people showered him with presents. Two suits would suffice for summer, and when he gained weight, Isabel could let them out so he could get another five years' wear out of them. He provided for his family, contributed to a wide variety of charities, and took pleasure in treating his friends generously.

In 1934 Gertrude Stein came from France to give a series of lectures on English literature; she had not returned to her native country for over three decades. Wilder invited Stein and her companion, Alice B. Toklas, to stay in his apartment while they were in Chicago. Stein and Wilder struck up a friendship that lasted until her death in 1946; during the years to come she would often importune him to collaborate with her on her next book. He always graciously avoided the requests, but tirelessly championed her writing and wrote introductions for three of her books.

A New Sense of Freedom

Assuming that his seriously ill father would die soon, Thornton announced in April that he would quit his teaching position at the University of Chicago on September 1, 1936. Although Amos Wilder had suffered several strokes and was severely incapacitated, to everyone's surprise he stayed alive through the winter and spring. His death on July 2 offered Thornton a new perspective on his own life. Many of Thornton's comments and personal letters indicate that he felt compromised and humiliated by his father's stern and unyielding personality. Hence, by the fall of 1936 Thornton felt a great sense of relief; he was now free from the teaching duties that often robbed him of his energy to write and from the burdensome influence of his overbearing father. To regain his emotional equilibrium, he decided to travel and devote himself to writing several long plays that had been bouncing around in his mind.

Late in 1936 Thornton went to New York City to discuss his literary ideas with the American writer Edward Sheldon, who at the height of his popularity suffered a stroke that left him blind and osteoarthritis that crippled him. To Thornton and many other writers of the time, Sheldon was a source of literary advice; he offered encouragement and sound judgments concerning the quality and potential of new material. Stretched out on his bed with a black satin linen over his face, Sheldon listened to Thornton excitedly outline a new play that he was writing called *Our Village*, which Thornton would eventually title *Our Town*. Thornton acknowledged later that Sheldon provided insightful suggestions and made a meaningful "contribution to the content of the play."

Encouraged by Sheldon, Thornton returned to the MacDowell Colony, where he rewrote the first act and made significant progress on the second and third. He may have finished the work by the summer of 1937, but he interrupted his writing to serve as an American delegate to the Eighth Institute for Intellectual Cooperation sponsored by the League of Nations. While in Paris for the conference Thornton visited his good friend Gertrude Stein. Her love of literature and awareness of literary trends inspired Thornton and motivated him to continue his writing with new energy. Indeed, many of Stein's literary theories and ideas about the form of writing helped shape Thornton's work.

Excited about finalizing *Our Town*, Thornton traveled to Zurich, where he secluded himself as the only guest at the Hotel Belvoir, five miles outside of the city. It was the perfect place to organize his thoughts; he took solitary walks in the woods, read books and newspapers, and ate leisurely meals on his balcony overlooking Lake Zurich. At forty years old, this respite seemed to focus his concentration and revitalize his creativity. From Zurich, Thornton wrote a letter to Gertrude Stein in which he rejoiced

> I am writing the most beautiful little play you can imagine. Every morning brings an hour's increment to it and that's all. But I've finished two acts already. It's a little play with all the big subjects in it; and it's a big play with all the little things of life lovingly impressed into it.

At one point while writing *Our Town*, Thornton was visited by a friend of Gertrude Stein, Samuel Steward, a young teacher at a prestigious Catholic college who had written a rather mediocre novel. Over the course of Steward's three-day stay, the two enjoyed each other's company by taking long walks, discussing literature, and reflecting on life, particularly the young scholar's future. Thornton, suffering from a mild case of writer's block at the time, was struggling to find a good way to open act 3 of *Our Town*. During one of his walks with Steward, circumstances triggered a creative inspiration. Midway during the walk it began to rain, and both men, wet and slightly miffed, complained of not having their umbrellas. The next morning while Steward slept, Thornton wrote the memorable opening scene of the third act where the crowd of mourners is standing at the grave site under umbrellas. Much of *Our Town* is drawn from Thornton's experiences and the people he knew. Although no character or setting is identical to any particular person or place, elements of Thornton's family and friends find their way into some of the characters, and Grover's Corners is reminiscent of the village of Peterborough, New Hampshire, the site of the MacDowell Colony. By mid-September 1937 Thornton wrote another letter to Gertrude Stein informing her that he had completed his play *Our Town*.

THORNTON'S RELATIONSHIP WITH JED HARRIS

Thornton mailed several scenes from his play to Jed Harris, the hugely successful Broadway producer-director who had shown an interest in Thornton's early work. Harris, who was in London at the time, wrote back, "I am most anxious to see you or speak to you on the telephone. Can you come to Paris for a few days?" Two days later Harris wired Thornton again: "Am very anxious to get on with *Our Town* and if I could have the script Monday morning I would have it typed in Paris before going back to America." Thornton agreed. In Thornton's opinion, Jed Harris was bold and audacious enough to stage the playwright's unconventional play. Thornton believed that Harris would understand the play's unusual elements, including that it lacked scenery, broke time sequence, and employed a stage manager as a character.

When Thornton arrived in New York in early December 1937 Harris had the playwright sequestered in a fancy Long Island cottage so he could make the necessary dramatic adaptations and revisions that Harris requested. At first Thornton willingly reworked his play, believing that the director was the one who could transform *Our Town* from a script to a forceful production. But once rehearsals began, Thornton was stunned to find that Harris continued to cut, adapt, and add to the drama. Thornton's trust in Harris was weakened by a growing apprehension that Harris really did not understand the play and that his alterations were weakening its power.

Apprehension turned to open hostility after the play's trial run at Princeton's McCarter Theatre in January 1938. The sold-out audience and the critics did not respond warmly to the presentation. *Our Town* received an unflattering review from *Variety:* "It is not only disappointing but hopelessly slow. Jed Harris has endowed it with a superlative cast, headed by Frank Craven, and it will probably go down as the season's most extravagant waste of fine talent." Thornton was enraged and accused Harris of flawed direction stemming from the director's overly nostalgic interpretation of the play. Unruffled by Thornton's outburst, Harris moved *Our Town* to the Wilbur Theater in Boston, where it opened on January 25, 1938, and languished for a disappointing week: Attendance was poor; the reviewers were, for the most part, indifferent or negative; and the production lost a sizable amount of money, over $10,000. The relationship between Thornton and his director grew steadily worse. On the first of February Thornton wrote a letter to Gertrude Stein in which he lamented that

> It's been one long fight to preserve my text from the interpolations of Jed Harris and I've only won fifty percent of the time. The play no longer moves or even interests me; now all I want out of it is money. . . . The play may be a failure. The whole blame of my state rests at Jed Harris' door.

OUR TOWN IS A SUCCESS

After the discouraging experience in Boston, Harris had trouble finding a theater in New York that would accept the play.

Eventually, he had to settle for a one-week run at the empty Henry Miller Theater. The day of the opening, February 4, seemed to be burdened with omens of an impending disaster. At 3:00 in the afternoon, for example, the Stagehands Union called to inform Harris that union rules required him to hire two more stagehands and that no actor could carry furniture, despite the fact that the script calls for actors to carry furniture onto the stage. Furious, Harris employed the extra stagehands, and shortly before the performance he caught one of them moving a chair. Harris instructed the hand to put the chair down and when he refused, the director exploded, "Why, you slimy, contemptible oaf, you ignorant pediculous loafer, you untalented, worthless, parasitical bloodsucker, I'll give you one more chance to put the chair down." Harris then hauled off and knocked the stagehand unconscious. If that was not tense enough, as the curtain was rising, Evelyn Varden, the actress who played Mrs. Gibbs, fainted in her dressing room and was revived only minutes before she had to enter the stage.

Despite the play's short history of failure and the stormy relationship between the author and the director, *Our Town* was well received. The audiences at the Henry Miller Theater were genuinely moved by the play, and, for the most part, the New York reviewers understood that Thornton's unconventional techniques opened possibilities for a new direction in modern American theater. Because of the agreeable response, the play was given a four-month run at the prestigious Morosco Theater on Broadway. Its stay there was moderately successful, playing to adequate but not sold-out crowds. Still the reviews were promising, and on May 2, while Thornton was in Tucson, Arizona, working on another play, *The Merchant of Yonkers*, *Our Town* won the 1938 Pulitzer Prize. With the Pulitzer announcement, audience attendance swelled and the play was extended through the summer and into the fall. Toward the end of its run Thornton agreed to take the place of actor Frank Craven as the Stage Manager. Thornton stipulated, however, that he would attempt the part only if Jed Harris was not in the theater while he was onstage. Most reviewers wrote that Thornton did an admirable job as an actor, and some even liked his interpretation of the character better than Frank Craven's.

ONGOING POPULARITY OF *OUR TOWN*

Soon after the play's run on Broadway, the publishing house of Samuel French printed and sold over 300,000 copies of the play. In the published version of *Our Town* Thornton removed many of the changes that he had made for Jed Harris. *Our Town* became one of America's best-loved plays. Revived many times, the play continues to touch a resonant chord within the people who see it.

In 1939 Hollywood producer Sol Lesser bought the film rights to *Our Town* for $35,000. Although Thornton turned down Lesser's request to write the screenplay, he did meet with the writers for six grueling days to outline a script. Despite being very cautious about making any significant changes for the film adaptation, Thornton did allow one major alteration. The playwright agreed to Lesser's request for a "happy ending" by having Emily live. Thornton rationalized the change by stating that "insofar as the play is a generalized allegory, she dies-we die-they die; insofar as it is a concrete happening it's not important that she die."

The writers who worked with Thornton, Harry Chanlee and Frank Craven, were paid significant salaries for the six-day script summit, but Thornton told Lesser that he really did not need any compensation. Lesser, who thrived in a world of expenses and profits, was surprised and touched by Thornton's generosity. For Christmas that year, Lesser sent Thornton a beautiful Chrysler convertible, delivered to Thornton's home wrapped in a huge red ribbon. Although Thornton saw the Lesser gesture as generous, it was not very practical since Thornton did not know how to drive and he did not have a driver's license. Lesser arranged a gala opening for the film in Boston on May 22, 1940. The movie played successfully all across America.

THE SKIN OF OUR TEETH AND *THE MATCHMAKER*

World War II had begun in 1939, and soon after the Japanese bombed Pearl Harbor in December 1941 Thornton chose to join the military; he was commissioned a captain in the air force. He had a few weeks before he had to report, so when Alfred Hitchcock asked for his help on the script for *The Shadow of a Doubt*, he traveled to Hollywood for intensive sessions with the great director. Hitchcock was so impressed with his work that he rode the train with him back to Washington, discussing the screenplay all the way. Between 1942 and 1948 Thornton was stationed in Europe and in Africa. During this time, the playwright became intensely interested in the existential writings of Soren Kierkegaard.

He also met and became friends with Jean-Paul Sartre, an existentialist novelist and playwright. Later, in 1948, Thornton would translate Sartre's drama *The Victors*.

Thornton's own play *The Skin of Our Teeth* opened just before he was to go overseas. The horrific events of World War II formed the backdrop for Thornton's hopeful message that humanity will endure even against impossible odds. The play's success was staggering, drawing sell-out crowds almost every night it was performed at the Plymouth Theater on Broadway. Most critics applauded it as a production with great flair and influence. Only a few critics attacked it for using what they considered to be theatrical novelties and for unsuccessfully dealing with the problem of evil.

However, just one month after its opening on November 19, 1942, Henry Morton Robinson and Joseph Campbell published an article in the *Saturday Review of Literature* in which they accused Wilder of drawing heavily from James Joyce's *Finnegan's Wake*, stating that *The Skin of Our Teeth* "is not an entirely original creation, but an Americanized re-creation, thinly disguised." The article sent shock waves through the literary community by implying that Thornton had plagiarized. The playwright weakly defended the charge by simply stating that critics should read the two works and make up their own minds. Despite the controversy, the play, which remained popular with audiences, won the Pulitzer Prize in 1943.

After the war, Thornton went back to work: teaching and lecturing, writing, even acting occasionally. He not only acted as the Stage Manager in *Our Town* but he achieved success playing Mr. Antrobus in *The Skin of Our Teeth*. Thornton's teaching, perhaps enriched by his wartime experience and his continued success as a writer, resulted in the Charles Eliot Norton Professorship of Poetry from Harvard for his brilliant discussions of Thoreau, Poe, Whitman, Dickinson, and Melville. Other awards followed, including the 1952 gold medal for fiction from the American Academy of Arts and Letters, the 1963 U.S. Presidential Medal of Freedom (the first year the award was given for distinguished civilian service in peacetime), and the 1968 National Book Award for *The Eighth Day*.

In 1954 Thornton achieved another extraordinary success in drama. Sixteen years after he first presented his unsuccessful farce *The Merchant of Yonkers*, Thornton rewrote it as *The Matchmaker.* The play was directed by the British director Tyrone Guthrie, and Thornton's friend Ruth Gordon played the lead role of Dolly Levi. The drama was a huge success in New York and the reviews were pleasant and laudatory. Audiences responded enthusiastically to the play's amusing elements of mistaken identity and character horseplay. The lightness of the production made it a perfect choice for a musical adaptation, a 1964 blockbuster entitled *Hello Dolly!* This Broadway musical earned Thornton more money than all his other works combined.

THORNTON'S LAST WORKS

Thornton continued to write. In 1967 he isolated himself from the frantic pace and flurry of his celebrity life and wrote a lengthy book entitled *The Eighth Day.* The novel incorporates virtually all of Thornton's ideas and ruminations on life that he had touched on previously. These are pulled together under the expansive theme that behind the mutability and seemingly inexplicable vagaries of life there exists a great design. Thornton states this theme at the end of the novel when he writes that "history is one tapestry" and that most humans cannot see broadly enough to understand that the whole encompasses the many small pieces of life. Although *The Eighth Day* won the National Book Award, most critics have subsequently dismissed the work, criticizing its forced characterization, artificially contrived situations, and didactic moral passages.

In 1973 Thornton, age seventy-six, published his last novel, *Theophilus North.* Although the work was not critically bashed, it was received quietly and with reservations by the reviewers. *Theophilus North* is much less pretentious than *The Eighth Day*, written more to entertain than to instruct. Because of this, the novel, advertised heavily by its publisher, survived on the best-seller list for more than twenty-one weeks and was enjoyed by Thornton's readership.

Thornton did not live to see the publication of the play he had been working on since before the Second World War, *The Alcestiad;* it was published posthumously, two years after his death. On December 22, 1975, in its transitions column, *Newsweek* magazine offered an obituary for Thornton Wilder, who had died on December 7; "Exit the Stage Manager" was written by Bill Roeder in the style of *Our Town.* It ended this way:

He was getting up in years at the age of 78. Still, it was a jolt for us folks in Grover's Corners—and I'll bet for a whole lot of other people, too—when Thornton Wilder slipped away with a heart attack during his afternoon nap the other day. God rest him. H'm—11 o'clock in Grover's Corners. You get a good rest, too. Good night.

PLOT AND CHARACTERS

Our Town covers twelve years, beginning in the morning and ending at night. As audience members use their imagination to visualize the setting, they begin to absorb a feeling for the movement of life in the small town of Grover's Corners. The first act introduces the audience generally to the town and specifically to two main families. In the second act these families are joined together in marriage as the son from one marries the daughter of the other. But in the third act they are separated by death. The play then is a zigzag journey through time, orchestrated by the Stage Manager, in which the audience becomes a participant in the merging of three realities: the reality of the play and its world of Grover's Corners, the reality that audience members bring individually to the theater, and a larger reality found in the overall pattern of life itself.

ACT 1

At the outset the audience is greeted with a stage setting that lacks a curtain and scenery. The solitary figure of the Stage Manager enters the stage, casually dressed and smoking a pipe, and, when everyone settles down, he begins by telling the audience the particulars of the production: the playwright, the director, and the cast. After providing the exact geographic location of the town, he identifies its layout: the mountain forming the backdrop of Grover's Corners, the tracks and railway station, the public school, a few important buildings, and the location of the various churches. As the Stage Manager moves downstage, he identifies two imaginary houses belonging to the play's two main families, the Gibbses and Webbs. It is early morning and the town is still asleep.

As the town awakes, the Stage Manager makes comments about various townspeople as they go about their early morning business. The audience sees Mrs. Webb entering her kitchen and Doc Gibbs "comin' back from that baby case." Doc Gibbs stops and talks to the eleven-year-old newspaper boy, Joe Crowell Jr. The Stage Manager, breaking the normal flow of time, tells the audience that Doc died in 1930 and Joe, who graduated from Massachusetts Tech. at the head of his class, died in France during World War I. The audience begins to feel the pulse of the town as Howie Newsome comes down Main Street delivering the milk. He stops and chats with Doc Gibbs and later with Mrs. Gibbs. Mrs. Webb calls upstairs to her daughter, Emily, to wake up for school. In short, Grover's Corners begins as it has countless days before, another ordinary day. There is nothing remarkable about the scene. There is hustle and bustle, a little gossip, and the recognition that this day will not be much different from any other.

The Stage Manager interrupts a conversation between Mrs. Gibbs and Mrs. Webb, thanks them, and then alerts the audience that he is going to skip ahead a few hours. He asks Professor Willard, an anthropology teacher from the State University, to explain the town's origin. Afraid that the professor is going to be a little long-winded and dry, the Stage Manager cuts him off and turns the audience's attention to Mr. Webb, the publisher and editor of the Grover's Corners *Sentinel*, the local paper. Mr. Webb sorts the town's residents into political and religious camps. The editor draws the conclusion that Grover's Corners is a "very ordinary town, if you ask me. Little better behaved than most. Probably a lot duller." Bridging the invisible wall between the stage and the auditorium, the Stage Manager asks the audience if they have any questions to ask Mr. Webb. An actress identified as the Woman in the Balcony asks a seemingly impromptu question about drinking in the town. Another audience plant, the Belligerent Man, asks, "Is there no one in town aware of social injustice and industrial inequality?" and a third, the Lady in the Box, asks about cultural pursuits in Grover's Corners. Mr. Webb's responses are simple, reflecting common folks living ordinary lives.

The Stage Manager returns his attention to the townspeople: "It's early afternoon. All 2,642 have had their dinners and all the dishes have been washed." George Gibbs strolls down the street and stops to converse with Emily Webb, who is picking flowers at the gate of her house. George, a high school classmate of Emily's, was impressed by the wonderful speech Emily made in school. He notes how hard she studies and how bright she is. George tells Emily that he wants to be a farmer. When George leaves, Emily informs her mother that "I'm going to make speeches all my life." Prompted by her conversation with George, she asks her mother if she is pretty. The future of both of these young people will intersect.

The Stage Manager stops the action once more to explain that a new bank building is being constructed and that he is "going to have a copy of this play put in the cornerstone and the people a thousand years from now'll know a few simple facts about us." It should tell the people of the future that "this is the way we were: in our growing up and in our marrying and in our living and in our dying." Music is heard from the choir practice at the Congregational church, directed by Simon Stimson.

It is evening now and the first act ends with a cross section of activity reflecting life and relationships: George and Emily discuss their math; Doc Gibbs raises George's allowance, but scolds him for not doing his chores; Mrs. Gibbs is sweetly chastised by Doc Gibbs for gossiping about the town drunk, Simon Stimson; Mrs. Gibbs worries that her husband is working too hard; and George pensively looks out the window while his kid sister, Rebecca, pesters him. The moon bathes them in light, and Rebecca asks her brother if the moon could crash into the earth. Rebecca expresses her wonder of it all when she questions George, "Is the moon shining on South America, Canada and half the whole world?" Rebecca tells George about a letter that Jane Crofut received addressed "Jane Crofut; the Crofut Farm; Grover's Corners; Sutton County; New Hampshire; United States of America . . . Continent of North America; western Hemisphere; the Earth; the Solar System; the Universe; the Mind of God—that's what it said on the envelope." Act 1 successfully contrasts daily life in one particular place in the world, Grover's Corners, with the larger cosmic background of the whole world, the relentless flow of time, and the universe.

ACT 2

The Stage Manager, who has been sitting on the stage throughout the intermission, begins the second act by telling the audience that three years have passed: Babies have been born, some townsfolk have lost the spring in their step, and others have fallen in love and gotten married. He informs everyone that this act is called "Love and Marriage."

As Howie Newsome delivers the milk, his pleasant conversation with various townspeople indicates that George Gibbs, one of Grover's Corners's finest baseball players, is about to marry Emily Webb. Meanwhile, in the Gibbses' home the morning of the wedding, Mr. and Mrs. Gibbs express concern over their boy marrying so young, but they ultimately conclude that "people are meant to go through life two by two. 'Tain't natural to be lonesome." George wakes and goes immediately to the Webb household, hoping to see Emily. Mr. Webb explains the custom that the groom cannot see the bride on the wedding day, and he advises George to be open with his thoughts and share his life with Emily.

The Stage Manager cuts the scene and offers to show the audience how George and Emily came to know they were meant for each other. He asks the audience to recall when they were young and first in love, when "you were like a person sleepwalking, and you didn't quite see the street you were in, and didn't quite hear everything that was said to you." The Stage Manager sets a flashback to Mr. Morgan's drugstore as George and Emily enter, both juniors in high school. Emily accuses George of being conceited and stuck-up. George thanks her for her openness and then admits his love for her and how he plans to forgo agriculture school, hinting that he wants to build a life with Emily.

The Stage Manager, who assumed the role of Mr. Morgan, the druggist, halts the scene again to set the stage for the wedding. As stagehands arrange the pews of the church, the Stage Manager, acting as the minister, preaches that a wedding is a sacrament that has been reenacted by millions, a ritual linked to the past and humanity's ongoing search for stability. The wedding party enters, and George, walking down the aisle of the theater, receives some catcalls from classmates dressed in their baseball uniforms. The Stage Manager scolds them, and George, shaken, is reminded of the youth he is leaving; he reflects on his marriage and his passage into manhood: "Ma, I don't want to grow old. Why's everybody pushing me so?" But George soon "regroups" as Emily enters. She too is frightened: "I never felt so alone in my whole life." The ceremony is performed by the Stage Manager, and at its completion he reminisces about the cycle of life:

The cottage, the go-cart, the Sunday-afternoon drives in the Ford, the first rheumatism, the grandchildren, the second rheumatism, the deathbed, the reading of the will,—Once in a thousand times it's interesting.

In this ritual of the wedding there is a uniting, a celebration of human activity. The townspeople join together and the two families are united. The Stage Manager announces that the second act is over and ten minutes will be afforded for intermission.

ACT 3

During the second intermission, stagehands arrange chairs onstage to represent twelve graves. The dead sit quietly and speak in a matter-of-fact manner, without sentimentality. The Stage Manager begins, "This time nine years have gone by, friends—summer, 1913." He is on a hilltop cemetery overlooking the town; the beauty of nature surrounds him. He points out some of the dead, Mrs. Gibbs, Simon Stimson, and Wallace, Mr. Webb's boy. Pondering philosophically, the Stage Manager suggests, "We all know that *something* is eternal, and that something has to do with human beings. . . . There's something way down deep that's eternal about every human being." Death is part of the cycle of life, and it is death that makes life meaningful.

An early arrival to the funeral, Sam Graig, Emily's cousin, converses with Joe Stoddard, the undertaker, about village residents who have died: The audience learns that Mrs. Gibbs is dead, that Simon Stimson committed suicide, and that today's funeral is for Emily, who died giving birth to her second child. Hence, the play begins with a birth, the "baby case" handled by Doc Gibbs, and runs full cycle to end with Emily's baby. Townspeople enter to attend Emily's funeral, carrying umbrellas because it is raining slightly. As the mourners gather around the grave site, the dead comment on the proceedings. Mrs. Soames, who had attended Emily's wedding, summarizes their feelings: "My, wasn't life awful—and wonderful." Suddenly, Emily appears from among the umbrellas. Somewhat dazed she greets Mrs. Gibbs and Simon Stimson and the rest of the dead. Over the protests of Mrs. Gibbs, Emily decides that she wants to relive one day of her life. Mrs. Gibbs pleads with her, "At least, choose an unimportant day. Choose the least important day in your life. It will be important enough." Emily picks her twelfth birthday.

The ubiquitous Stage Manager directs Emily back fourteen years to the morning of February 11, 1899. Emily sees her mother in the kitchen and her father as he enters, returning from a speaking engagement. Overcome, Emily says, "I can't bear it. They're so young and beautiful. Why did they ever have to get old?" Emily turns away and laments to the Stage Manager, "I can't. I can't go on. It goes so fast. . . . Take me back—up the hill—to my grave." Emily expresses the central theme of the play when she asks, "Do human beings ever realize life while they live it?—every, every minute?" Simon Stimson, the pessimist, responds, "That's what it was to be alive. To move about in a cloud of ignorance; to go up and down trampling on feelings of those . . . of those about you. To spend and waste time as though you had a million years." But Mrs. Gibbs admonishes Simon, telling him that he does not see the whole truth. An unknown man from the dead puts the situation in a larger context by referring to the stars and the millions of years it takes for some light to get to the earth. The audience is left with a confluence of two aspects of life: the mutable and brief journey of life replete with happiness and pain, birth and death, and love and lonesomeness; and the awareness that there is something eternal, something vast, and something meaningful in existence. The Stage Manager ends the play by drawing a dark curtain across the scene and stating that "Most everybody's asleep in Grover's Corners." He merges the world of the play with the "real" world of the audience one last time as he tells them that it is late, eleven o'-clock in Grover's Corners, the same as "real" time in the theater. He bids them farewell and suggests they get a good night's sleep.

INTRODUCTION TO CHARACTERS

Since the characters' words and actions are not precisely individualized, the characters are frequently hard to distinguish from one another. They often appear as animated figures who populate Wilder's diorama of small-town America, long since gone. The twenty-two townspeople who pass across the stage are types rather than individuals, created by the playwright to express ideas, allegorical figures portraying abstract human qualities and representing the universal struggle to find meaning and significance in the journey from birth to death. Although Emily and George pass through identifiable traits of the maturation process, their essential characters do not significantly change from the beginning of the play to the end. Nevertheless, taken as a whole, the characters emerge collectively as a viable and sensitive portrayal of humanity, one that provokes most audience members to assess their own sense of self.

THE STAGE MANAGER

The Stage Manager is the narrator of *Our Town*. Although Wilder does not specify his age or how he should look, his dialogue indicates that he is mature and soft-spoken, and he presents himself as a country philosopher. He is dressed casually, wears a hat, and smokes a pipe, and his speech is colloquial, often with a wry sense of humor. He never comes across as pretentious and he never misleads; there is little that is cryptic, sinister, or derisive about him. At times in the drama he speaks directly to the audience; he moves props like a stagehand; he makes comments about the characters; he establishes the scene; and he even assumes a few roles, most notably the preacher and Mr. Morgan, the druggist.

Although he appears simple, his role in the drama is multifaceted and complex, for it is through him that the action of the play pushes forward and characters are understood. He is the direct connection between the audience and the people of Grover's Corners. In fact, at one point in the first act he takes questions from actors in the audience, directly bridging the invisible wall that normally separates the actors from the spectators.

The Stage Manager is also a guide through the imaginary world of Grover's Corners. He creates the scene in the mind's eye of the audience members and explains to them details about characters and place: "This is our doctor's house,—Doc Gibbs'. This is the back door. There's some scenery for those who think they have to have scenery." He can also manipulate time, pushing the action into the past or future. Early in the first act, for example, he interrupts the scene and tells the audience, "Now, we'll go back to the town. It's early afternoon."

The Stage Manager also functions as a Greek chorus making comments about the nature of the characters and their actions. For instance, at the wedding he provides insight into the nature of the ceremony and how the characters feel about it: "This is a good wedding, but people are so put together that even at a good wedding there's a lot of confusion way down deep in people's minds and we thought that that ought to be in our play, too."

By the end of the play, the Stage Manager's words not only apply to the characters of Grover's Corners but take on a universal quality, depicting insights into the nature of humanity. When Emily asks her crucial question near the end of the play, "Do any human beings ever realize life while they live it?" the Stage Manager seems to assume the voice of the playwright when he answers, "No. The saints and poets, maybe—they do some." The rest, sadly, allow life to go by unappreciated.

EMILY WEBB

Emily's function in the play is twofold: First, she epitomizes a typical American girl who must face the normal challenges of growing up, and second, she serves as an important spokesperson for the essential message of the play.

Like all young women, Emily must advance through the normal stages of maturation. As a young adolescent in the first act, Emily has typical conflicting feelings about herself. On the one hand she is enthusiastic about her studies and her own abilities. Indeed, she is one of the smartest students in school, telling her mother at one point, "I made a speech in class today and I was very good." On the other hand, Emily, like most schoolchildren, expresses self-doubt, "Am I pretty enough . . . to get anybody . . . to get people interested in me?"

In the second act Emily moves through another phase of maturation as a teen in love, somewhat shy and annoyed that she is not receiving enough attention from the young man she loves, George. She initiates her expression of love by admonishing George for neglecting her, telling him, "I don't like the whole change that's come over you in the last year." She forces herself to tell him that he is spending all his time at baseball and never speaks to her anymore. At the end of act 2, George and Emily get married. Naturally, Emily has qualms about this big step in her life; on the morning of the ceremony, she blurts out to her father, "But, Papa,—I don't want to get married."

In the final act, the audience learns that Emily has died in childbirth. Through conversation of both live characters and dead, Wilder relates that Emily's adult life was a success: She was a competent mother of her first child, a fine wife, and she and George created a reasonably loving life together. But now that she is dead she understands that, while she was alive, she failed to appreciate what life meant. Emily requests to go back from the dead and observe a day of her life, her twelfth birthday. The experience is agonizingly painful. She asks the dead if "human beings ever realize life while they live it." She wants to know if humans ever have time to look at one another, or are they simply blind? Emily's comments express Wilder's fundamental message that human beings fail to understand the beauty of life while they live it, that even the most common aspects of life have meaning and an element of the eternal in them.

GEORGE GIBBS

Like all the characters in *Our Town*, George is nothing more than a type, an average American boy living a normal, day-to-day existence. Like all young men, he must move through difficult stages to discover his manhood.

In the first two acts, George displays the typical youthful traits of most adolescents: He likes sports and is one of the best baseball players in Grover's Corners; he is a good boy but does not always do his chores, resulting in a mild scolding from his father for not chopping wood for his mother; he is a decent brother but is at times annoyed with his kid sister, Rebecca, telling her, "you're always spoiling everything"; he is sometimes too full of himself, and Emily has to tell him, "you've got awful conceited and stuck-up, and all the girls say so"; he struggles academically at school, but he is popular and is elected senior class president; and he has goals for his life, hoping to take over Uncle Luke's farm.

In the second act George moves out of childhood when he recognizes that he loves Emily and subsequently, upon high school graduation, marries her. His movement to maturation, symbolized by the wedding, is not done without the usual doubts. Just before his marriage he complains to his mother, "Ma, I don't want to grow old." But Mrs. Gibbs cuts him short, "No, no, George,—you're a man now." And so George gives himself to society's expectations; he upholds his bargain as a man and marries Emily. Their wedding ceremony brings act 2 to a close.

Although he has only a brief appearance in act 3, the audience understands that George embodies the normal sequence of life: childhood innocence, school, a passage to manhood, marriage, work, procreation, joy and suffering, loss and recovery. George's life has progressed as millions of other lives have unfolded before him. At the end of the play, George suffers the loss of Emily; he struggles to her grave and falls full length, stricken with grief. One of the dead responds disapprovingly by saying, "He ought to be home." George, like countless others who have suffered, will eventually regroup and return home to take care of his two children.

THE WEBB AND THE GIBBS FAMILIES

The two main families in the play are not distinguished for their unique characteristics but are developed to show that the human experience has notable similarities. Both fathers are engaged in professional work that puts them in touch with a broad spectrum of humanity: Mr. Gibbs is a family doctor, and Mr. Webb is the editor of the newspaper. Both have hobbies: Doc Gibbs involves himself with the study of the Civil War, and Mr. Webb is a student of Napoleon. Both of the mothers are deeply involved in the daily maintenance of their families. Mrs. Gibbs likes to plan fancy trips, and Mrs. Webb works in her garden. Rebecca is the kid sister of George, and Wally is the kid brother of Emily. Both families face some unexpected loss: Mrs. Gibbs dies of pneumonia, and Wally Webb dies suddenly of a burst appendix.

The purpose of matching the two families is to demonstrate that most average people lead lives with similar values, hopes, experiences, and pain. They are not intended to be identical, but they are meant to share the common bond of being human, authentic people who are taking their turn at life's journey.

CHAPTER 1

The Format and Theatrical Principles of *Our Town*

READINGS ON
OUR TOWN

Wilder's Experimental Approach to Theater

Ima Honaker Herron

Ima Honaker Herron suggests that Wilder's inventiveness as a playwright was apparent in his early works, particularly his one-act plays. Wilder revolutionized modern stage presentation by experimenting with a sceneless stage, imaginary props, flexible jumps in time sequence, pantomime, and a stage manager as a character. Herron argues that together these devices in *Our Town* effectively and powerfully emphasize the playwright's dominant theme—the essential dignity of the human spirit. According to Herron, *Our Town* is a creative twentieth-century morality play that traces the life journeys of ordinary people and, at the same time, memorializes a way of American life that has disappeared.

Ima Honaker Herron was a professor of American literature at Southern Methodist University. She is the author of *The Small Town in American Drama* and *Better College English.*

Among the more experimental modern playwrights who have created vivid community images to counterbalance those of the "uglified" town and the alluring city, Thornton Wilder has successfully brought into theatrical focus memorable small places, past and present, in New Hampshire, New York, and New Jersey. His daring departures from conventional realism in stories, novels, and plays have stemmed both from his unusually original mind and from his international upbringing, which afforded him wide acquaintance with humanity. The shaping influences on his art have been many. His New England parents, his birthplace (Madison, Wisconsin), his boyhood schooling in Hong Kong, Shanghai, and later in California, his youthful service in the

Excerpted from Ima Honaker Herron, *The Small Town in American Drama* (Dallas: Southern Methodist University Press, 1969). Reprinted by permission of the author's estate. *Endnotes in the original have been omitted in this reprint.*

Coast Artillery Corps, his college years at Oberlin, Yale, and Princeton, and his archeological studies in Rome all helped foster in him an unusual detachment and freedom from entangling coteries (though it is true that for a while the New Humanists did regard him as their "golden boy"). A self-reliant thinker, Wilder has explored in his studies the cultures of various epochs and lands, discovering in them different manifestations of a favorite theme: the essential dignity of the human spirit. Apparently the timeliness of such a theme has had much appeal for him. In *The Skin of Our Teeth* the Fortune Teller, speaking about Man's sleeplessness because of worry about his past, asks of Sabina: "What did it mean? What was it trying to say to you?" She warns: "If anybody tries to tell you the past, take my word for it, they're charlatans!" Nevertheless, in his various forms of fiction, Wilder has tried repeatedly to tell the past, often dramatizing it in its relation to the disorders and confusions of the present.

WILDER'S INVENTIVENESS

Wilder began his rather curious career with novels, *The Cabala* (1926) and the Pulitzer Prize–winning *The Bridge of San Luis Rey* (1927); yet the drama had always fascinated him, even in adolescence. In his preface to a collection of early one-act plays, *The Angel That Troubled the Waters* (1928), he notes that he composed the first of more than forty one-acters when he was only fifteen. These "three-minute plays for three people" were followed by a second group published in 1931 as *The Long Christmas Dinner and Other One Act Plays.* Although little more than youthful "literary exercises in compressed expression," these playlets reveal his bent toward experimentation as well as his efforts "to capture not verisimilitude but reality." His portrayal of a stage manager in "Pullman Car Hiawatha" and "The Happy Journey from Trenton to Camden" foreshadows the more ingeniously employed Stage Manager who chattily directs the action in *Our Town.* Also, in "The Happy Journey" he experimented with some success in creating illusion on a sceneless stage. This family sketch reveals his ingenuity in stimulating the imagination to supply both scenery and properties on a bare stage. Ordinary chairs serve as the Kirbys' Chevrolet, while a cot suffices for the indoor furnishings. A repetitive pattern appears in "Pullman Car Hiawatha," in which straight chairs are substitutes for berths.

"The Long Christmas Dinner," describing the Bayard family's Christmas gatherings over a period of ninety years, involves time as a potent force which so fascinated Wilder that his experimentations with that motif extended to *Our Town*, *The Skin of Our Teeth*, and other later fiction. In this playlet the directions for costuming and stage business emphasized Wilder's early striving for a new method. The eating of imaginary food with imaginary knives and forks, as well as the use of wigs of white hair and of shawls, adjusted simply and at indicated moments to suggest the aging of the Bayard women, reflects the young playwright's inventiveness. His growing displeasure, during the twenties and earlier, with what he derided as the "soothing quality" of popular plays—of tragedy without "heat," of comedy lacking "bite," and of social plays without a code of "responsibility"—may have motivated his portrayal of Roderick as an exasperated critic of the town which the Bayards, with their factory assets, helped control. "Great God," Roderick exclaims, "you gotta get drunk in this town to forget how dull it is. Time passes so slowly here that it stands still, that's what's the trouble." Finally, in his dramatic writing at Yale in 1919, when as editor of the *Yale Literary Magazine* he serialized his first play, *The Trumpet Shall Sound*, Wilder gave clear foreshadowing of his later efforts to become, as he once said, "not an innovator but a rediscoverer of forgotten goods and . . . a remover of obtrusive bric-a-brac in the theatre."

However charade-like these early playlets were, they quickened the maturing of Wilder's originality. As the thirties lengthened and he turned more and more toward the theater, Wilder shared in common with other insurgent playwrights a dislike for the "ridiculous, shallow, and harmful" plays which then dominated the commercial theater. Like Maxwell Anderson and Eugene O'Neill, he began in earnest to experiment with the dramatic expression of poetry and imagination, combined with enough realism to bring his plays in touch with the everyday world. Fortunately his development as a playwright coincided with a time of crusading zeal in the theater, in both Europe and the United States. Inspiration for a new theatrical course which was to give strong competition to Broadway's commercialized offerings came from many sources. The emergence of progressive producers like Arthur Hopkins; of the Theatre Guild, Eva Le Gallienne's Civic Repertory Theatre, the Playwrights' Company, and other art groups; of original stage designers, such as Jo Mielziner, Lee Simonson, and Robert Edmond Jones; of gifted actors able to respond to fresh and original roles in the new expressionistic, or constructivistic, plays; and of imported imaginative foreign plays like Hungarian Ferenc Molnar's *Liliom* (1921) and Karel Capek's Czechoslovakian fantasy, *R.U.R.* (*Rossum's Universal Robots*), produced in New York in 1922, contributed greatly to the revitalization of our native drama and theater.

Wilder's temperamental distaste for the popular sentimental play, with its pseudo-realistic terms, and for doctrinaire realism, which conventionally represents the surfaces of life with photographic fidelity, influenced his experimentation with unusual dramaturgic methods. He turned toward the creation of effective patterns of feelings and emotions. The aesthetic principles of repetition and variation, of manners and customs indicative of the passage of time, of dramatic portrayal by unrealistic and nonrepresentational techniques, and of contrasting emotions to avoid monotony all appealed to his imaginative mind. It is no wonder, then, that his best-known and most successful original play, *Our Town* (1938), has been termed a "New England allegory," "a beautiful evocative play," "a tender idyll," "a hauntingly beautiful play," and "less the portrait of a town than the sublimation of the commonplace."

In this appealing play Wilder, largely through the medium of a folksy and interlocutory Stage Manager, shows himself as a whimsical philosopher of the commonplace. Re-creating three periods in the history of Grover's Corners, a placid New Hampshire town, he transmutes, as Brooks Atkinson wrote in the *New York Times*, "the simple events of human life into universal reverie" and gives "familiar facts a deeply moving, philosophical perspective." Eschewing what his generation deemed the ultimate in theatrical art—the box set and the convention of the fourth wall—Wilder chose to stage his play without scenery and with the curtain always raised. By stripping his play of everything extraneous, he succeeded in giving a profound, strange, and unworldly significance to the simple life of a remote New Hampshire township from around 1901 to 1913. Wilder himself, however, has written that he did not offer *Our Town* "as a picture of a New Hampshire village; or as a speculation about the conditions of life after death . . . ," an element which he confesses to have borrowed from Dante's *Purgatory*. Rather, he regarded this play as "an attempt to find value above all price for the smallest events in our daily life." To dramatize and universalize the significance of life's minutiae, he set Grover's Corners against "the largest dimensions of time and place." As he has said, his trick of repeatedly using such words as "hundreds," "thousands," and "millions" tended to universalize Emily Webb's happiness and sorrow—to attune her algebra exercises, her twelfth birthday celebration, and her youthful love for George Gibbs to similar experiences of teen-age girls everywhere.

THE CREATIVE STYLE OF *OUR TOWN*

Though an original and stylized drama, *Our Town* presents the life ritual—the plain, uneventful life in a New Hampshire village—through relatively simple action. Timed for certain days in the serene era of the Mauve Decade, the play shows two young neighbors—George Gibbs, son of a kindly doctor, and Emily Webb, whose father edits the Grover's Corners *Sentinel*—growing up amidst a friendly circle of parents, George's sister Rebecca, Emily's brother Wally, neighbors, schoolmates, and townspeople in general. As the first act begins the audience sees a half-lighted empty stage, devoid of either curtain or scenery. Soon the easy-going Stage Manager, "hat on and pipe in mouth," comes on stage and begins to address the spectators in a folksy, friendly manner. (This role was superbly enacted by Frank Craven when the play began its New York run at the Henry Miller Theatre on February 4, 1938.) While he chats about the time—dawn on May 7, 1901—and the history of the town and township, the Manager acts in the dual role of property man and *raisonneur* [a wise man or commentator]. He pushes into place a few chairs, tables, ladders, and planks, which with two arched trellises make up the only realistic properties. Serving as a one-man chorus, he genially comments on the plan of the town, with its Polish Town across the tracks as well as its Main Street. After identifying the churches, the town hall, the post office, and the stores, he describes the Gibbs and Webb families, their homes, the neighbors, and local affairs in general. As the action progresses he answers questions asked, from time to time, by the spectators, actually actors planted in the audience, who quiz him about the town's culture and its attitudes toward social injustice, inequality, and drinking. On occasion he assumes the roles of minor characters, male and female.

The organic structure of the almost plotless three acts has frequently been analyzed in relation to the ways in which Wilder telescoped births, everyday living, deaths, and time. Basically each act is structured on the double plan of a street scene followed by an enactment of family life within either the Gibbs or the Webb household. In each street scene the folksy conversation, involving a milkman, a newsboy, a constable, and various other citizens, helps build up an atmosphere of neighborliness and explain the homely nature of each family group. Thus the first act, after a spotty tracing of local history and a review of one full day of community activity, portrays the ordinary routine in the two adjoining homes in which George, played by John Craven, and Emily, played by Martha Scott, are growing up. From this act onward most of the stage business is through pantomime, as when Dr. Gibbs, returning home after an early morning call, "sets down his—imaginary—black bag" and Mrs. Gibbs, busy in the kitchen, goes "through the motion of putting wood in the stove, lighting it, and preparing breakfast." Acts II and III, again offering a combination of street and family scenes, with a final scene at the town's hillside cemetery, have a new focus: the courtship and the marriage of George and Emily and Emily's death in childbirth. Throughout the play Wilder, by abandoning scenery and relying to a great extent on nonexistent properties, tried to revive some of the Elizabethan techniques which gave greater importance to the actor, unencumbered by realistic scenery and properties.

WILDER'S PORTRAYAL OF ORDINARY PEOPLE

The somberly toned third act, a poignant scene in the graveyard above the town, takes place on a rainy day in the summer of 1913. Umbrella-laden townspeople have climbed the hill to attend the burial service for young Emily. Here, as throughout the action, the real protagonist, as [American critic] Edmond Gagey has shown, seems to be the town of Grover's Corners, with an emerging narrative thread expressing the happiness, and now the sorrow, of a young farm couple over a period of nine years. As Emily joins Mother Gibbs and other townsfolk in the graveyard, these community dead appear indifferent to what is still happening in the town below. As the Stage Manager comments,

"They get weaned away from the earth" and are waiting for "the eternal part in them to come out clear." In the conclusion the relationship between life and eternity also touches upon everyday living and its potentialities, the latter too often tragically overlooked by many. Emily's last speech, which gives a moving re-creation of her happy experiences on her twelfth birthday, philosophically implies as much. As the vision of this birthday fades, Emily sobs, "We don't have time to look at one another. . . . Oh, earth, you're too wonderful for anybody to realize you. Do any human beings ever realize life while they live it?—every, every minute?" The play ends as casually as it opened. The Stage Manager announces that it is late evening and though "most everybody's asleep in Grover's Corners," the stars are still "doing their old, old criss-cross journeys in the sky." Then he draws a dark curtain across the scene.

Thus imbued with homeliness of action and characterization, *Our Town*, the Pulitzer Prize play for 1938, is reminiscent of the pilgrimage depicted in *Everyman*. As a twentieth-century morality play, it traces the journeying of ordinary people, telling, without sensationalism, "the way we were . . . in our living and in our dying." It reveals Wilder's creative use of the theater. And, as he has said, it was written "out of a deep admiration for those little white towns in the hills. . . ." Further, it memorializes—and idealizes—the hill-encircled and custom-bound village of Grover's Corners as a type of once flourishing and neighborly American village now vanished from our national scene. In Wilder's words, it presents "the life of a village against the life of the stars."

Wilder's Dramatic Principles

M.C. Kuner

According to M.C. Kuner, Wilder perceives drama as an art of collaboration that depends on the combined efforts of actors, directors, designers, and many others. Kuner also notes that Wilder rejected realistic characterization and used characters as symbols to deliver a message. Wilder believed that drama should move beyond the perpetual present of a play and thus he uses the Stage Manager in *Our Town* to break the boundaries of the past and the future. Kuner writes that Wilder expounded the theory that the use of theatrical conventions and pretense, like masks and metric verse, worked to provoke the audience's imagination. Finally, Wilder supported the notion that drama is a collective experience rooted in ritual and celebration.

Kuner argues that Wilder's theatrical principles come together in *Our Town* to convey effectively the abstract idea that all people are bound together in a vast common experience because they share certain similar thoughts and actions. Wilder, like the Italian dramatist Luigi Pirandello, struggled to free theater from its physical limitations to liberate the imagination of the audience.

Drama critic and playwright M.C. Kuner is a professor of English at Hunter College in New York. She wrote *Capacity of Wings* and received Stanford University's Anderson Award for Playwriting.

A few years after *Our Town* was produced Thornton Wilder drew up some principles that, he believed, defined the drama. They serve so admirably as the backbone for all his plays that they make a useful introduction to them.

Excerpted from *Thornton Wilder: The Bright and the Dark*, by Mildred Kuner. Copyright © 1972 by Mildred Kuner. Reprinted by permission of HarperCollins Publishers, Inc.

WILDER'S PRINCIPLES OF DRAMA

Wilder stressed, first of all, the fact that the theater was an art that demanded many collaborators and therefore needed intervening "executants"—that is, actors, directors, and designers upon whom the interpretation would depend. Thus he mentioned a production of [Shakespeare's] *The Merchant of Venice* that was played with a maximum of sympathy for Shylock; yet Wilder himself recalled a performance he had seen in which the great French actor Fermin Gémier presented Shylock as a vengeful and hysterical buffoon, while Portia was a *gamine* from the Paris streets. Both points of view are equally interesting, both equally valid. Therefore, for Wilder,

> Characterization in a play is like a blank check which the dramatist accords to the actor for him to fill in—not entirely blank, for a number of indications of individuality are already there, but to a far less definite and absolute degree than in the novel. . . . The dramatist's principal interest being the movement of the story, he is willing to resign the more detailed aspects of characterization to the actor.

Although his example of *The Merchant* does not really prove his case, for Shylock is not an abstract but a very sharply drawn character, the argument tells us something about Wilder's notion of theatrical characterization. Just as he rejected the realism of the depression-oriented novel, he rejected the realism of detailed portraiture such as Eugene O'Neill was giving the American theater in plays like *Desire Under the Elms.* Bertolt Brecht had reduced his characters to deliberate symbols in order to enhance the political beliefs he held; Wilder used the same means to clarify his religious beliefs. In any theater that is essentially didactic the characters are obviously less important than the message.

Another theory that Wilder propounded was that the action in a play "takes place in a perpetual present time. . . . Novels are written in the past tense. . . . On the stage it is always now." In addition, the novel has the advantage of an omniscient author who can tell his readers facts that the other characters do not know; on a stage everything must be presented between the characters. Wilder pointed out that the Greek Chorus performed just such a function in the theater, and he believed that the modern playwright had to find an equivalent—as he was to do in supplying the Stage Manager for *Our Town.* A play thus provided with a Stage

THE STATIC NATURE OF *OUR TOWN*

*In his May 29, 1938, article entitled "Stage Aside: From
Thornton Wilder," in the* New York Herald-Tribune, *critic
Lucius Beebe quotes Wilder's description of* Our Town *as static
and unconventional.*

"I now consider myself a playwright rather than a novelist,"
Mr. Wilder said. "Indeed, my life has really been one long ap-
prenticeship to the theater. And, for that matter, I have yet to
write my first real conventional play. *Our Town* evades every
possible requirement of the legitimate stage. It is pure description, entirely devoid of anything even resembling conflict, expectation or action, which are usually considered the component
parts of any play. The only other drama in all literature that I
know of that is as static as *Our Town* is *The Trojan Women*,
where the various characters come on the stage, speak their
piece and move utterly nowhere. I've completely exhausted the
possibilities of this particular pattern. Any other play I write will
have to be more active. The next one, in fact, will deal primarily
in arousing the curiosities of the audience."

Narrator attains a kind of timelessness, for the narrator can
be part of the play's momentary action and yet be a commentator on what has happened in the past; or he can look
into the future and tell the audience what he sees, for he is
both enclosed in finite time and stands beyond, outside it. Finally, if he can move back and forth in time so freely, he
must be aware of the repetitions of history and the ideas that
flow from one century to the next, and so he becomes a
transmitter of myth, legend, allegory. In such a theater the
characters are analogous not to the planets, which "wan-
der," but to the stars, which are fixed; while the background
or setting, like the earth itself, moves in time.

Observing that the theater is a world of pretense, Wilder
enumerated such conventions as the playing of women's
roles by men in the Greek (and Elizabethan) age; the use of
metric speech, although in life people do not speak verse;
the reliance on masks and other devices. And he argued that
these conventions did not spring from naiveté but from the
vitality of the public imagination: they provoked the audience into participating instead of having all the work done
for them by the dramatist. Even more important, in Wilder's
estimation, the action was thereby raised from the specific to
the general. In Shakespeare's world Juliet was not a "real"

girl living in a "real" house cluttered with "real" furnishings; she was played by a boy on a bare stage and so became not a particular person but all the star-crossed heroines who have ever lived and who will live in the future. By Wilder's definition, theatrical pretense is absolutely essential to reinforce his theories of time.

Because drama is a collective experience, in Wilder's words, because it appeals to the "group-mind," it has about it the excitement of a festival, a coming together to celebrate an event. And so ritual must be part of drama in some fashion. It may be based on a typical evening during a particular season of the year, like "The Long Christmas Dinner." The details of the ritual are not important, but it must have enough familiarity about it to be recognizable as a convention to the audience. Equally, the material must be broad enough in scope to reach a large number of people *simultaneously*, and this need demands a subject-matter that is common to ordinary experience.

OUR TOWN AS THE CULMINATION OF WILDER'S DRAMATIC PRINCIPLES

Our Town is, therefore, the blossoming of Wilder's theories. Emily and George are types rather than individuals, outlines rather than photographs. Although the play begins in America's past (between 1901 and 1913), it deals with the future, too. For in the end, Emily, having died, comes back to visit Grover's Corners; she exists simultaneously in all three pockets of time. The Stage Manager constantly reminds us of the make-believe quality of the play by asking us to imagine this or that prop; he himself plays different roles in addition to his own; he is not limited by sex, since he takes the part of Mrs. Morgan as well as of other men in the town; and from time to time he comments on the weather or the state of the world, lectures to the audience, and interprets the actions of the characters for us. Wilder even succeeds in supplying us with ritual: the hum of activity that makes up everyday life. One might almost say that brushing one's teeth or one's hair is a ritual; Wilder picks up moments like these to affirm that all of us are bound together in one vast chain, because we all share certain common thoughts and actions. There is a moment in James Joyce's *Portrait of the Artist* when Stephen thinks about God, who, he knows, is called "Dieu" in French, and God can always tell the nationality of the boy praying to Him by the language that is used. The mere idea of a French boy offering a simple prayer to "Dieu" (whose real name is God anyway, Stephen asserts), while at the same time an Irish boy is praying in *his* own language and so on across the universe, is enough to give Stephen a headache, for where does infinity end? But it is exactly this feeling that Wilder is after: we are all one in the One. As one of his characters in *Our Town* says:

> I never told you about that letter Jane Crofut got from her minister when she was sick. The minister of her church in the town she was in before she came here. He wrote Jane a letter and on the envelope the address was like this: It said: Jane Crofut, The Crofut Farm; Grover's Corners; Sutton County; New Hampshire; United States of America.

When the other character wants to know what is funny about that, the girl answers:

> But listen, it's not finished: the United States of America; Continent of North America; Western Hemisphere; the Earth; the Solar System; the Universe; the Mind of God—that's what it said on the envelope. . . . And the postman brought it just the same.

And the other character comments, "What do you know!". . .

PIRANDELLO'S INFLUENCE ON WILDER

Certainly in *Our Town* and in his other plays Wilder showed a link with [Italian dramatist Luigi] Pirandello. The latter had attempted to liberate the conventional stage from its physical limitations by centering much of the action in the minds of the characters and by juggling such opposites as madness and sanity, falsehood and truth, illusion and reality, always asking which was which. Pirandello's is a theater where nothing is absolute or fixed, where everything is relative and fluid; and even when he sets his plays in a parlor his imagination lifts the spectator far beyond the room itself. This latter aspect of his work, its open-ended quality, most suggests what Wilder was trying to do. Added to the didacticism of Brecht and the freedom of Pirandello is another element in *Our Town*, the idea behind William Blake's quatrain:

> To see a World in a Grain of Sand
> And a Heaven in a Wild Flower,
> Hold Infinity in the palm of your hand
> And eternity in an hour.

Our Town as Allegory

Donald Haberman

Donald Haberman maintains that Wilder intended the characters in *Our Town* to stand not as individuals, but as symbols to convey ideas. Hence, Haberman concludes that Wilder's generalized characterization requires the members of the audience to create the characters in their imagination.

Haberman writes that *Our Town* is an allegory akin to a medieval *Everyman* play. Consistent with the conventions of allegory, characterization is absent except to distinguish abstract qualities like love or lust. As a result, Emily and George are not meant to be distinct individuals, but rather are intended to function as a "young girl" and "young boy." Similarly, Haberman reasons that the wedding in the play, like the birthday, is designed not to be a specific celebration, but a generalized one that allegorically outlines the behavior patterns of a human celebration. In this sense, the wedding transcends Emily and George and becomes everybody's wedding. Haberman concludes that the delineation of a distinct wedding with particular details and individual motivation is not Wilder's purpose; instead, it is the idea of a wedding that is important.

Donald Haberman is a professor of English at Arizona State University, Tempe. He is the author of *G.B.S.: A Bibliography of Writings About Him* and a contributor to *Four Quarters,* a now defunct literary magazine.

Characterization and narration, in Thornton Wilder's theater, are inextricably bound. The two are related not merely as a matter of being consistent to a single style; their unity and Wilder's use of it determine the style, for his practice is to give over psychological characterization in favor of an arbitrary and artificial arrangement of events.

Excerpted from Donald Haberman, *The Plays of Thornton Wilder: A Critical Study;* © 1967 by Wesleyan University. Reprinted by permission of Wesleyan University Press.

In "Some Thoughts on Playwriting" Wilder defined his goals in characterization.

> Imaginative narration—the invention of souls and destinies—is to a philosopher an all but indefensible activity.
>
> Its justification lies in the fact that the communication of ideas from one mind to another inevitably reaches the point where exposition passes into illustration, into parable, metaphor, allegory, and myth.

Characters, therefore, are created to convey ideas, and they will naturally make their appearance as symbols.

Gertrude Stein in *Narration*, for which Wilder wrote the introduction, explained how the arbitrary, imaginative creation of characters was superior to relying on the facts.

> Vasari and Plutarch are like that, they make them up so completely that if they are not invented, they might as well be they do not really feel that any of the ones about whom they tell had any life except the life they are given by their telling. That can happen and when it does it is writing.

Wilder converted this idea of Gertrude Stein's, that the characters are more real when they are imagined, from narrative prose to theatrical writing; he left the characterization so general that the people in his plays must really be created in the imagination of the audience, although, of course, the play contains characters, and actors must play them.

The first manuscript version of *Our Town* is particularly emphatic in its special treatment of characterization. The Stage Manager played all the children but Emily and George. In addition, he played Simon Stimson and, as in the final version, Mrs. Forrest and Mr. Morgan, the druggist, as well as the minister who marries George and Emily. The audience was required in this version to imagine not merely the particulars of characters but also their very presence. Wilder felt it necessary at least once to tell the audience what he was doing. The Stage Manager says, "Now I'm Mr. Morgan in front of his drugstore." This was later removed, and the Stage Manager simply took the speeches of Mrs. Forrest and Mr. Morgan without any fuss, and the roles of Stimson, Rebecca, and Wally were given to actors.

Our Town as Allegory

Wilder depends very heavily on his audience for much of the work that has been traditionally expected from the playwright himself, but he derives advantages from this kind of writing. In one of the letters to Sol Lesser, who produced the filming of *Our Town,* concerning whether or not Emily should die, Wilder distinguished between the stage and the film.

> In a movie you see the people so *close to* that a different relation was established. In a theatre they are halfway abstractions in an allegory; in a movie they are very concrete. So insofar as it's a concrete happening, it's not important that she die; it's even disproportionately cruel that she die.

This short comment reveals much about Wilder's concept of his own work. First, he views *Our Town* as an allegory, probably as something like a twentieth-century *Everyman.* One of the important qualities of allegory is that characterization is absent, except when it serves to distinguish abstract qualities, such as hate or lust. Wilder recognizes that his own characters fit the situation of allegory in that they are "halfway abstractions." Emily and George represent, only as much as it is absolutely necessary, two individuals. Their chief function is to be a young girl and a young boy.

This kind of characterization determines what happens on stage. It is the reason why a complete marriage proposal is not presented. Emily and George do not have personalities sufficiently distinct to participate in so individual a procedure. When anybody marries, his wedding is much like that of anybody else. Anybody's *deciding* to marry and *proposing* is one and one and one. Each proposal is different from the rest, and most frequently, as a result, marriage proposals are an event for comic dramatization.

THE ALLEGORICAL SIGNIFICANCE OF THE WEDDING

The wedding ceremony is a thing altogether different. The occasion itself, the ceremony, like the occasion of the birthday in Act III, carries with it advantages to Wilder's allegory. First, both are the kind of event about which everybody has a ready-made memory. Secondly, the witnesses of such events are called together without any particularization. Wedding guests behave pretty much the same at one wedding as at another. People weep at weddings; they are happy at birthdays. Each celebration comes equipped with a behavior pattern which is available to the entire audience, and it is independent of George and Emily.

Wilder has not offered simply a wedding. In the real world most people require some personal interest in the bride or groom to make their wedding interesting. In the theater a different situation exists. Again in a letter to Lesser, Wilder wrote:

> My only worry is that—realistically done—your wedding scene won't be interesting enough, and that it will reduce many of the surrounding scenes to ordinaryness. . . .
>
> On the stage with *Our Town* the novelty was supplied by
> (1) economy of effect in scenery.
> (2) the minister was played by the Stage Manager.
> (3) the thinking-aloud passages.
> (4) the oddity of hearing Mrs. Soames' gabble during the ceremony.
> (5) the young people's moments of alarm. . . .
>
> —And for a story that is so generalized [the danger of dwindling to the conventional] . . . is great.
>
> The play interested because every few minutes there was a new bold effect in presentation-methods. . . .
>
> I know you'll realize that I don't mean boldness or oddity for their own sakes, but merely as the almost indispensible reinforcement and refreshment of a play that was never intended to be interesting for its story alone, or even for its background.

Wilder knew that neither the plot nor the *mise en scène* [setting] was intended to be interesting. This is a partial answer for those people who were enchanted by the story of a typical New England town. Also the wedding of an Emily Webb and a George Gibbs is scarcely the point, for the wedding is everybody's. The unusual staging retained the interest in an event which takes place essentially with people who are not people at all, but ideas.

One of Lesser's letters to Wilder illustrates what might happen to *Our Town* if insistence on detail and private motive were applied.

> It has been suggested for movie purposes a means to be found to attach the third act to circumstances already within the play. . . . By this it is meant that perhaps there should be a problem affecting the married life of Emily and George growing out of the differences in their mentalities. I cite the following only as an example:—
>
> Emily is brighter than George; in her youth she has the best memory in her class—she recites like "silk off a spool"—she helps George in his mathematics—she is articulate—George is not—she is "going to make speeches all the rest of her life.". . .
>
> Query: Could it be Emily's subtlety in the soda-fountain scene that causes George to make the decision not to go to Agricultural School? The audience gets this, but George feels it is his own voluntary thought. He makes the decision not to go.

Could Emily, after death, re-visit her fifth wedding anniversary . . . and now see her mistake?

Emily in life is likely to have been overambitious for George, wanting him to accomplish all the things he would have known had he gone to Agricultural School, but which he has had to learn mainly by experience. In a single sentence we could establish that George did not develop the farm as efficiently and as rapidly as Emily thought he should have. She continued to get ideas out of newspapers and books, as she did out of her school books, and had tried to explain them to George, but he was slow in grasping them. She had been impatient very often. Someone else's farm may have been progressing faster than George's and she may not have liked that. . . .

Now she sees this. She remembers she was responsible for his not going to Agricultural School. She has overlooked many of George's virtues—she took them all for granted. All this was her mistake. . . .

Could there be a great desire to live, to profit by what she has just seen, rather than go back to the grave—should she long to live—would the audience, witnessing this picture, pull for her to live—and she does?

. . . It would only change the expression of your philosophy, not the philosophy itself, which would be retained.

Lesser's suggestions indicate that he lacked any real understanding of the play. His final comment—"it would only change the expression of your philosophy"—suggests that he does not understand any plays at all. His emphasis is on event for its own sake, and his plan is rather like the scenario for a soap opera.

Wilder answered Lesser with restraint, but firmly:

I feel pretty concrete about trying to dissuade you against showing Emily returning to her fifth wedding anniversary and regretting that she had been an unwise wife.

(1) It throws out the window the return to the 12th birthday which you feel is sufficiently [*sic?* insufficiently] tied up with the earlier part of the picture, but which is certain of its effect.

(2) It introduces a lot of plot preparation in the earlier part of the picture that would certainly be worse than what's there now. Scene of George running the farm incompetently. Scene of Emily upbraiding him.

(3) It makes Emily into a school-marm "improving" superior person. The traits that you point out *are* in her character . . . but I put them there to prevent her being pure-village-girl-sweet-ingenue. But push them a few inches further and she becomes priggish.

(4) The balance of the play, reposing between vast stretches of time and suggestions of generalized multitudes of people

requires that the fathers and mothers, and especially the hero and heroine, be pretty near the norm of everybody, every boy and every girl.

If this is made into an ineffectual-but-good-hearted-husband and superior-interfering-wife, the balance is broken.

It's not so much new "plotting" that is needed, as it is re-freshing detail-play over the simple but sufficient plot that's there.

George and Emily, individually psychologized and motivated, would tumble into another one of those hopelessly stupid stories of boy and girl, and a dull one at that.

Our Town as an American Myth

Thomas E. Porter

Thomas Porter maintains that *Our Town* reflects the
power of myth in modern drama. Unlike many
dramatists of his day, Wilder forgoes realism and
presents mythic elements directly. Wilder uses ritual
techniques to universalize space and time and reduce individuals to types and action to categories to
express the American myth of equality and the common man.

According to Porter, Wilder designs Grover's Corners to represent the ideal of the rural community and
the family unit on which it is built. This ideal image
avoids sentimentality and cliché because of Wilder's
ritual method of presentation. In short, Porter argues,
Wilder is working to present the truth of a myth and a
vision of the ideal life. Hence, it is idealism, not realism, that Wilder seeks.

Thomas E. Porter is a professor of English at the
University of Texas at Arlington, where he teaches
modern drama and is the dean of Liberal Arts.

Our Town has a theatrical quality that distinguishes it from
[other plays of its time]. Wilder uses no scenery and no act-
curtain. The play begins with an announcement by the Stage
Manager that is calculated to draw attention to the bare
stage and to insist on the audience's consciousness of its role
as spectator. No realistic props are used, the Stage Manager
steps into the action from time to time and reads bit parts,
lapses of time and flashbacks are announced and commented on. Moreover, there is no "hero" in the conventional
sense, no central figure on whose decision the plot pivots. In
fact, there is very little plot. The play presents the daily life
of a small town over some seventeen years. The dramatis

Reprinted from *Myth and Modern Drama*, by Thomas E. Porter (Detroit: Wayne State
University Press, 1969), by permission of the Wayne State University Press.

personae are not memorable; they have no qualities that carry them beyond the soap-opera stereotype. According to the canons of the "well-made play" or even of modern expressionism, *Our Town* is a pretentious, sentimental collection of clichés. Yet the play was well received on Broadway in 1938 and continues to hold a fascination for American audiences. Brooks Atkinson gave this tribute to its impact:

> By stripping the play of everything that is not essential, Mr. Wilder has given it a profound, strange, unworldly significance. There is less a portrait of a town than the sublimation of the commonplace; and in contrast with the universe that swims around it, it is brimming over with compassion. Grover's Corners is a green corner of the universe.

The untraditional devices, the presentational, non-realistic mode have received considerable attention, but their overall significance needs further investigation. For *Our Town* approaches pure ritual in method and illustrates, in a unique way, the power of the myth in modern drama.

WILDER'S MYTHIC EXPRESSION

[Other] playwrights have used the myth as substructure and have filled out the pattern with specific incidents and individual personae. By elaborating the structure with "realistic" character motivations and concrete incidents, they fixed the action in time and space to give it the appearance of reality. This "realistic" treatment, to a greater or less degree as the play approaches "slice-of-life" naturalism, conceals the mythical structure and makes it serve the life-like details. The play is then once removed from the myth, and each author can find his own way of realizing it. This "realistic" dramatic mode may be described in classical terms as the involution of the universal (myth) in the particular. Its method involves: 1) adding a locale and a temporal dimension, 2) giving the characters precise motivations, 3) filling out the categories of the pattern with concrete episodes that are causally related to the motivations. To the pattern of the myth the playwright gives a local habitation and a name. This is the most common mode of "imitation" in modern Western drama.

It is possible to deal with the myth more directly, to express a complex of attitudes in a non-realistic mode. This kind of drama will necessarily have strongly ritual characteristics. It is commonly accepted that myth and rite are expressions of the interpretations that a community puts upon archetypal experiences like birth, maturity, death or purgation, and initiation. As myth is the verbal expression of these interpretations, ritual is their interpretation in action. Because it is an interpretation of the archetypal, the ritual has characteristics that set it off from other actions whether actual or imitative. It takes place in a universalized space and time, that is, it does not happen "here" or "there," but at the center of the universe, in a space that includes all space; it happens in a "present" that includes all time. The actors in the ritual are not so much individuals as types: priest, chorus, victim. The action of the ceremony can be reduced to categories: separation, testing, communion, for instance, in initiation rites. These categories do not have any logical sequence nor is motivation expressed; one event follows the other because the archetype has it so. The playwright, then, can employ these ritual techniques without displacement if he chooses. This ritual, non-realistic technique tries to express the complex of attitudes that comprise the myth in its own terms, that is, as ideal interpretations of experience by the community. *Our Town* is a play that uses this technique, that expresses an American myth—the ideal of equality, democracy and meaningful daily life for the common man that emanates from a specifically American complex of attitudes—in a ritual mode.

OUR TOWN AS A MYTHIC AMERICAN COMMUNITY

The ideal with which Wilder is working is the rural community, the vision of small town life, a kindly, middle-class, democratic existence. As distant an observer as [French historian Count Alexis] de Tocqueville pointed to the New England township as the highest political form evolved by the Americans. "The township of New England," he wrote, "is so constituted as to excite the warmest human affections, without arousing the ambitious passions of the heart of man." Institutional freedom was honored by an unconscious ritual observance, and all extremes of class and wealth were leveled off into a golden mean. This image of the ideal community is little different from the image presented at the turn of the century by novelists like Booth Tarkington and Dorothy Canfield Fisher, and summarized by Vernon Parrington:

> (1) A land of economic well-being, uncursed by poverty and unspoiled by wealth; (2) A land of "folksiness"—the village a

great family in its neighborliness, friendliness, sympathy; (3) Primarily middle-class, and therefore characteristically American, wholesome and human in spite of its prosaic shortcomings; (4) The home of American democracy, dominated by the spirit of equality, where men are measured by their native qualities.

To adapt this image to drama Wilder found it necessary only to add the religion of the folk—a mild Protestantism that is integrated into the life of the town, an undogmatic faith that does not prescribe or proscribe, but meshes with the democratic aspirations of the people. The characteristics that de Tocqueville described in the 1830s and that Parrington enumerates a century later are exemplified point for point in Grover's Corners. The play gives dramatic shape to this vision of the ideal American community.

All the details in *Our Town* are typical of this ideal. The village lies in a valley at the foot of "our mountain." Main Street splits the town; its grocery and drug store are the focus of social life. There is the public school and the high school and a wide variety of churches: Congregational, Presbyterian, Methodist, Unitarian, Baptist "down in the holla' by the river," and Catholic "over beyond the tracks." The houses all have backyards and there is only light horse-and-buggy traffic on Main Street. Outlying farms add to the rural flavor. The people who live in Grover's Corners are, according to the editor of the town paper, "lower middle class: sprinkling of professional men." The political statistics and the form of government reflect a staunch conservatism within the democratic process: "eighty-six percent Republicans, six percent Democrats, four percent Socialists; rest indifferent." The town is run by a board of selectmen and all males vote at twenty-one. But economic status, politics and religion are not divisive factors; easy commerce between classes is taken for granted. Social and economic problems are handled on an individual level: "The citizens do all they can to help those who cannot help themselves and those that can they leave alone." The milkman and the constable and the newsboy each makes his own contribution to the running of the town—as do doctor and editor. Each is respected as an individual; each delivers his product to the neighbors with a sense of accomplishment in a spirit of friendly largess. There is no race-problem, no employer-employee agitation, no keeping up with the Joneses. Grover's Corners is a society conscious of its community, whose members are basically good.

Even the shortcomings of the town and its citizens are typical and generally simply provide an occasion for greater good. The town's life is rather dull—"Very ordinary town, if you ask me. Little better behaved than most. Probably a lot duller." Yet dullness does not discourage the young people, for they generally settle down there; in fact, serenity might be a fair synonym. The choirmaster's drinking offers the ladies an opportunity for innocent gossip and everyone a chance to exercise charity. The minister keeps him on at his work and even suicide does not excommunicate him. When a boy forgets to chop the week's wood supply, his father gives him a little talk, the essence of tact and common sense, leaving the boy thoroughly abashed and eager to redeem himself. The admitted lack of "culture" in the town is balanced by interest in, and attention to, nature—listening to birdsong and watching the sun rise over the mountain. These defects are the other side of the coin of American virtues: simplicity, regularity, compassion and kindliness.

THE ROLE OF THE FAMILY

The basic unit of society in Grover's Corners is the family. The community is constituted by families living together, working in tandem, intermarrying with neighbor's son or daughter. The play pivots around the lives of two typical families, the Webbs and the Gibbses. Each has two children, a boy and a girl. The identity of the adults is established primarily by their parenthood—they are Mother and Father, and their lives are focused here. They exercise a wise supervision over the children and their deep affection has a matter-of-fact gloss. Mrs. Webb and Mrs. Gibbs make good breakfasts, string beans, get the children off to school. Choir practice at the Congregational Church and mild gossip afterwards provides them a social outlet sufficient for Grover's Corners. They have little ambitions of their own—to see the ocean, to visit "Paris, France, where people don't talk English and don't even want to," but they are not really disturbed by their stability. Mr. Webb and Dr. Gibbs, professional men in the small-town manner, share their concern for their family with a concern for the town. The doctor knows his patients and sacrifices for all of them—he goes out on night calls in Polish town, then attends to Mrs. Wentworth's stomach trouble. When advisable, he enlists the aid of the neighbors in dealing with his boy; the constable checks on George's smoking. The editor picks up news items from the milkman and the constable and tries to keep mistakes in the paper at a minimum.

Son and daughter accept the world of their parents, and their own interrelationships are typical. George Gibbs' little sister Rebecca annoys her big brother with her presence and her questions; he tolerates her. When George prepares for his wedding, his little sister retires to her room and cries. George and Emily get along as athletic hero and the-girl-next-door should. They take one another for granted till that moment when they realize how they feel about each other. George typifies the red-blooded, good-hearted American boy; Emily is everybody's version of the girl next door. George respects his parents even though he sometimes forgets to chop wood for his mother, he is not very good at his studies, he captains the baseball team; he is honest, shy about showing emotion, devoted to his family. Emily is a good student, reasonably attractive, helpful to her mother, earnest with George. When they decide to marry, they are willing to settle down on a farm near town and make a life that will mirror their parents'. Like the town itself, there is nothing unusual about the personae except their consistent typicality.

Thus far the ingredients of Wilder's play resemble those of a thoroughly sentimental, idealized potboiler after the manner of Tarkington or Fisher. This is the American that Meredith Nicholson eulogized in *The Valley of Democracy*, that Sinclair Lewis satirized in *Main Street*, that H.L. Mencken stigmatized as the "booboisie." If Wilder had chosen to depict Grover's Corners "realistically," his play would have the same dated, tired quality that brands the small-town novel of the 20s. As it is, *Our Town* resembles no real town on hill or in valley; it corresponds to an ideal whose model exists potentially in the attitudes of every American. The theoretical expression of this ideal may take shape something like this:

> The individual feels himself to be a part of a social unity and harmony, which is regarded as the embodiment of universal and objective ideals and as a reflection of an ultimate harmony in nature. He finds emotional security and fulfillment, not through the assertion of his will against the natural and social environment, but through participation in the

processes of nature and in the collective enterprise of society. Yet in subordinating himself to the social order, he does not deify it or endow it with absolute and final authority. . . . The synthesis of individual will and social discipline, without which there can be no high civilization, is to be found not in intellectual formulas, but in the sentiment of patriotism, in moral and religious idealism, and (as Whitman declared) in "the manly love of comrades."

Living in "our town" includes a social unity and harmony with nature, the fulfillment of the individual within the community. It inculcates patriotism and moral principles and friendly social interchange. To be born into this community is to be born into the warm bosom of a family, to grow up there is to be nurtured by wise and affectionate parents and neighbors. To marry there means deepening the bonds of friendship into a closer tie and starting a new family that is the image of the one left behind. To die there means resting quietly among people you know and love. Though this image is ideal, the play escapes sentiment and cliché because of its mode of presentation. The ritual method makes all the difference.

WILDER'S PRESENTATION OF IDEAL TRUTH

Wilder is not unaware of the implications of his presentational technique. When he writes about the play and about playwrighting, the terms "myth," "fable," and "ritual" recur frequently. He is concerned with patterns, with the universals that the theatre can present:

> The theatre longs to represent the symbols of things, not the things themselves. All the lies it tells—the lie that this lady is Caesar's wife; the lie that people can go through life talking blank verse; the lie that that man has just killed that man— all those lies enhance the one truth that is there—the truth that dictated the story, the myth.

In "Some Thoughts on Playwriting" he indicates that his concept of myth and story goes beyond the details of narrative; myth, fable, story are patterns that address themselves to the "group mind."

> It rests on the fact that (1) the pretense, the fiction, on stage would fall to pieces and absurdity without the support accorded to it by a crowd, and (2) the excitement induced by pretending a fragment of life is such that it partakes of ritual and festival, and requires a throng.

In statements like these, Wilder echoes the findings of the Cambridge anthropologists and anticipates some of the critical theories of Northrop Frye. Wilder acknowledges that the "truth" with which the dramatist works is an expression of that complex of attitudes which exists in the mind of the community. The myth that he presents in *Our Town* falls into that category that Frye calls "apocalyptic"—myth operating at the top level of human desire.

> In terms of narrative, myth is the imitation of actions near or at the conceivable limits of desire. The gods enjoy beautiful women, fight one another with prodigious strength, comfort and assist man, or else watch his miseries from the height of their immortal freedom. The fact that myth operates at the top level of human desire does not mean it necessarily presents its world as attained or attainable by human beings. . . . The world of mythical imagery is usually represented by the conception of heaven or Paradise in religion, and it is apocalyptic, . . . a world of total metaphor, in which everything is potentially identical with everything else, as though it were all inside a single infinite body.

Our Town deals with the apocalyptic aspect in the American complex of attitudes—the vision of the ideal life, the aspirations of the community at their highest pitch. To represent this ideal plausibly, in a realistic context, would destroy its ideality; whether or not the apocalyptic is attainable in the practical order is irrelevant to the myth. The truth which Wilder is dealing with is the truth of the vision as apocalypse, as ideal; thus his mode of presentation is attuned to the vision.

Our Town as a Classical Tragedy

Arthur H. Ballet

According to Arthur H. Ballet, *Our Town* follows the
major precepts of classical Greek theater: The play
centers on the continuing cycle of living; the Stage
Manager, who links the play to the audience, serves
as a Greek chorus; and the setting is simple and
sparse. Ballet characterizes the play as a tragedy because, as Aristotle defines it, tragedy must elevate the
audience's awareness of life. *Our Town* does this
through the development of the young married
woman Emily, who is ennobled by death and is subsequently elevated to a higher understanding of life.

Ballet asserts that the greatness of *Our Town* has
been validated by the theater-going audience. Wilder's
play enjoys worldwide appeal. Ballet argues that this
popularity emanates from the play's sincere reflections on the inner strivings of the human spirit; its
simple but effective language; and its focus on the
very human concern of the inevitability of death.

Arthur H. Ballet was a professor of drama at the
University of Minnesota. He is the editor of the multi-
volume *Playwrights for Tomorrow: A Collection of
Plays*.

In the short history of American literary criticism, there has
been a continuous search for "the great American drama." It
is the purpose of this essay to continue this search by exploring the qualifications for this signal honor of Thornton
Wilder's *Our Town*. It is hoped that, since *Our Town* continues to be widely read and performed in educational and professional theatre, new light may yet be shed. . . . Either edu-
cators, directors, and the general theatre-going public have
been deceived by the play, or they must come to terms intel-

Excerpted from Arthur H. Ballet, "In Our Living and in Our Dying," *The English Journal*, vol. 45, May 1956, pp. 243–49.

ligently with it if they are to continue presenting it in the theatre or the classroom.

As a beginning, it might be observed that literary and moral implications assumed, all important drama in the history of the theatre has had popular appeal. Great theatre is neither closet drama, which is to be read effetely by connoisseurs, nor is it *avant-garde* drama, which is to be relished by bored or malcontent sophisticates. That drama which through the years has gained in literary and theatrical respect and security has always appealed to the then-current theatre-going audience. For example, the great plays of Sophocles not only won literary laurels but were *the* popular plays of their day, drawing on the entire citizen-population of ancient Athens. Likewise, Molière was both an actor and a playwright who knew how to succeed in the difficult art of pleasing a living, popular audience. And, of course, William Shakespeare's dramas were the "smash hits" of their own days. Elizabethan audiences and critics went so far as to view the Bard as a hack who turned out popular but unimportant plays for the general amusement. They looked elsewhere to now-forgotten dramatists for "great drama." However, it is not suggested that all popular drama is necessarily important or significant, but merely that great drama has been popular theatre.

Attention must be turned next to those playwrights who have appealed to the general American audience. The criterion that the drama must have stature, significance, and literary importance before it may be considered rules out long-run plays like *Tobacco Road, Life with Father,* and *Mister Roberts.* Four playwrights remain for consideration. Eugene O'Neill undoubtedly was the greatest of the American innovators and experimenters in the theatre. His finest plays, now that they may be viewed in perspective, seem to have been his "sea plays," which at best are fragmentary vignettes. His pretentious, longer attempts have been disappointing as literature and as theatrical fare. Second, Tennessee Williams has enjoyed almost unprecedented success as a playwright, but closer observation reveals that his best efforts have been devoted to a minute examination of neurotic Southern women. The resultant appeal seems to lie in Williams' sensitive and sensational portraiture without further implication or significance.

The third leading playwright is Arthur Miller, whose

rugged but "safe" social protest of the '40's and the '50's has undoubtedly been enormously popular in the theatre, but whose plays lose their significance when carefully examined for what they have to say. *The Death of a Salesman*, for example, has been justifiably called by one critic a "sententious snivel" rather than the significant American tragedy to which it has pretensions. All three playwrights seem to appeal to some segments, but they have not had the lasting and universal qualities which stir not only imagination but intelligent reflection as well.

The fourth playwright is Thornton Wilder, who, according to a recent poll of playwrights in *The Saturday Review*, is, interestingly enough, American dramatists' own choice as their favorite living playwright.

Where, then, is the appeal of Wilder's *Our Town*? Frank M. Whiting, in *An Introduction to the Theatre*, points out that the play has qualities beyond its novelty:

> . . . it is an honest and revealing portrait of small-town American life. It has been criticised as sentimental, but American life is sentimental; Emily, George, and the others give us a far more genuine insight into twentieth-century American living than do the studies of neurotics, gangsters, and sexually frustrated.

It is necessary, however, to go beyond this, to qualify "sentimentality," and to consider the play as a modern American tragedy. . . .

OUR TOWN AS CLASSICAL DRAMA

Our Town is a carefully constructed drama, following the precepts of classic drama with certain justified modifications. Actually it is a trilogy. Act One may be thought of as a separate play dealing with The Daily Life, Act Two examines Love and Marriage within the totality of its act structure, and Act Three expands the first parts of the trilogy into a complex of eternity where the mystery of life is culminated in death.

Like its Greek predecessors, *Our Town* is concerned with the great and continuing cycle of life; out of life comes death and from death comes life. This cycle is man's closest understanding of eternity, his finest artistic expression of what he senses to be a mission and a purpose. The trilogy, thus considered, admirably re-interprets this concept in modern terms and language and form, finding its roots in what is probably the finest drama of all time: Sophocles' *Oedipus Rex.*

The use of the stage manager as a chorus is another manifestation of close attention to the classic structuring of the drama. The chorus-stage manager serves as the human link with the audience and personifies the *milieu* of society. Joining the audience with the events presented in the spaceless and timeless stage, he explains and interprets, fills in, and establishes the background for each episode. He is, however, more than just a narrator. Abandoning the modern concept of the impersonal, almost mechanical commentator, Wilder has returned to the kind of choric voice so effective in Greek tragedy. The stage manager represents the observing community; he is biased, sympathetic, informed, and concerned. His calmness in the face of both joy and disaster is never construed into passivity. The most lyric passages of the play are assigned to him, and this is quite rightly conceived by the playwright, for, as the agent of the human community in the drama, what occurs within the play makes a difference and must be sensitively considered.

At the same time, the stage manager subtly introduces a note of patience and understanding which is essential if the action is to have a meaning above that of a sentimental or emotional orgy for the entertainment of the audience. His interruption of the action, his interspersed observations, and his serious but twinkling control of the progress of the play all serve to prevent over-identification, which would destroy the higher implications of the play.

Then, too, there is the classic simplicity of the setting. Left to the imagination, it avoids realism of time and place which would devoid the play of its larger application. Returning to a theatrical tradition ranging from Athens to Elizabethan England, it returns also to a plane of imaginative rather than realistic reproduction and soars above mundane distractions of actuality. In addition, and still within the classic tradition, Wilder employs asides, soliloquies, choric interludes, short scenes, and frank theatricalism to heighten and expand his basic theme.

Some producers of the play . . . have attempted to "enhance" the production by adding suggestive or stylized scenery. It would seem that they have failed to grasp the fundamental reason for Wilder's elimination of conventional scenic devices in the first place. It is not a trick or "gimmick" to make the play sensational; on the contrary, Wilder, like his classic predecessors, was aware of the inherent scenery of the theatre itself. He chose deliberately, and with great sensitivity to the whole meaning of his own play, to utilize the theatre as the setting, for he wished to examine theatrical reality. This is by no means an easy thing to do. The theatre is not reality, of course; it is a life of its own but only insofar as it is a selective, sensitive, active and reflective image of the world beyond the theatre's walls. Wilder was aware of this function of the theatre, and he has made use of it and accentuated it by eliminating scenic devices beyond the physical theatre itself.

OUR TOWN AS TRAGEDY

Still, none of these structural details are in themselves enough to enable one to call *Our Town* a tragedy. Aristotle, in his *Poetica*, established tragedy as a "purgation through pity and fear" and as an "ennoblement" as well as the picturization of the fall of a great man. At first glance, *Our Town* appears to fall short of such ambitious purposes. The very simplicity and "ordinariness" of the drama seem to make a mockery of higher purposes. There are, however, deeply significant actions beneath the surface which do indeed fulfill Aristotelian definitions.

Death is the fear-agent employed as a catharsis. The audience witnesses the fall of the smallest of God's creatures: a young mother who becomes aware of the tragedy of life, and who finally is ennobled by death to understand how wonderful life is:

> EMILY: Good-by, good-by, world. Good-by, Grover's Corners . . . Mama and Papa. Good-by to clocks ticking . . . and Mama's sunflowers. And food and coffee. And new-ironed dresses and hot baths . . . and sleeping and waking up. Oh, earth, you're too wonderful for anybody to realize you. Do any human beings ever realize life while they live it?—every, every minute?

> STAGE MANAGER: No. The saints and poets, maybe—they do some.

Tragedy, in its finest sense, need not and should not be "sad." It should rather be elevating, should point the way to a higher level of understanding of man as a creature revolving in the cosmos. By these Aristotelian standards, then, *Our Town* approaches significance as a tragedy.

WILDER'S MANIPULATION OF TIME AND PLACE

Wilder has, by careful dramaturgical manipulation of time and place, established the play quite properly in perspective. A few examples should illustrate this operation. In Act One, after the daily life has been exemplified in its simple dignity and zest, George and his younger sister, Rebecca, are sitting at night looking out of an upstairs window when Rebecca tells of a girl friend's letter from her minister:

> He wrote Jane a letter and on the envelope the address was like this: It said: Jane Crofut; The Crofut Farm; Grover's Corners; Sutton County, New Hampshire; United States of America; Continent of North America, Western Hemisphere; the Earth; the Solar System; the Universe; the Mind of God.

In Act Two, the stage manager stops the action of the wedding to reflect on the timeless eternity which surrounds man at each moment in his search:

> The real hero of this scene isn't on the stage at all, and you know who that is. It's like what one of those European fellas said: every child born into the world is Nature's attempt to make a perfect human being. Well, we've seen Nature pushing and contriving for some time now. We all know that Nature's interested in quantity; but I think she's interested in quality, too . . . and don't forget the other witnesses at this wedding—the ancestors. Millions of them.

And a final example of Wilder's time and space manipulation is the stage manager's soliloquy in the cemetery, opening Act Three. Time has passed, changes have been made, death and life have continued their endless cycle:

> Now I'm going to tell you some things you know already. You know'm as well as I do; but you don't take'm out and look at'm very often. I don't care what they say with their mouths— everybody knows that SOMETHING is eternal. And it ain't houses and it ain't names, and it ain't earth, and it ain't even the stars . . . everybody knows in their bones that SOMETHING is eternal, and that something has to do with human beings. All the greatest people ever lived have been telling us that for five thousand years and yet you'd be surprised how people are always losing hold of it. (After explaining that the actors sitting on stage in chairs are "dead" and that they are waiting, he continues.) . . . And what's left? What's left when memory's gone, and your identity, Mrs. Smith?

Not only is the issue joined directly to the audience, but the level of the drama aspires toward an ever-increasing expansion of the scope of the play as a statement of faith in the microcosm, Man.

THE APPEAL OF *OUR TOWN*

Assuming that audiences have been aware, however sub-consciously, of these complexities within the drama, they do not explain the enduring and affectionate appeal of the play. And it will be remembered that earlier in this examination the criterion of popularity as well as significance was established for determining "great drama." *Our Town* is *prima facie* a popular play; eighteen years of professional and amateur production have not dimmed its lustre as an audience-getter or its appeal as a drama to be read and studied in classrooms throughout the world.

Our purpose here is not to prove that the play is popular but to attempt to determine *why* it is popular. Lamentable though it may be, people do not go to the theatre to hear sermons or to be told that the only truth they can comprehend is that the end of all life is death and that in death they will achieve life. *Our Town* has other appeals, some immediately apparent and some quite deceptive. The daily life has the appeal of familiarity: school, with its triumphs and lessons to be learned; the routine of cooking meals and shelling peas; young, unselfish love in the village drugstore; human fear, as with George and Emily on their wedding day; and the homely verities of human existence, as when Dr. Gibbs confesses that on his wedding day he worried how he would ever find enough to talk about with his young wife. The familiarity of this daily life, as so expertly sketched in *Our Town,* releases the audience's skepticism and induces a sense of suspended disbelief. If *Our Town* does not reflect life as it really is, at least it suggests what the daily life should be like, and the audience approves.

Also present is the sentimentality already referred to, but it is without sententiousness; it has romance without romanticism, and innocence without naïveté. The fears and the faith reflected are without melodramatic trappings, and are sincere reflections of the innermost strivings of the human spirit. In short, they "ring true" because they are common experiences.

Attention finally must return to that quality which, however morbid its surface may seem, recognizes a quiet, resigned sense of justice in the inevitability of death itself. Throughout life, man is surrounded by this knowledge. In the play, old age, a burst appendix, childbirth, and alcoholism all contribute to the final end. But the audience is never repelled by this concept; it learns, as Emily must, to accept the life cycle, which not only is as it is, but is as it has to be and should be.

Any attempt to separate "content" or "theme" from "form" or "structure" is a purely academic one and seldom worth the effort. In any literature worthy of consideration at all, theme and structure are one and the same thing, determining each other. Questions of suitability and compatibility are largely matters of individual taste. With masterly strokes, Wilder has joined both the form and the content into an inseparable entity which both appeals and instructs. The audience engages in a struggle resulting both in pity and fear but ultimately culminating in an ennoblement through acceptance and understanding.

Thus, it would appear that *Our Town* is not only an important drama but also a significant one, for it has much to relate without pretentions. The "common folk" in the play very directly refute the concept of the mediocre average or perfect being. The simple yet effective language is appropriate not only to the characters involved but to the ideas expressed. The prose-poetry which Wilder has chosen is without the modern falsification of poesy. The dramatic conflicts and tensions are devoid of melodramatic clichés or the cinematic "happy endings" which betray life itself. There is no drama worthy of the name without conflict and action, but Wilder has elevated both of these ingredients. Life and death are part of a whole and yet in constant conflict, as are love and hate (witness the exquisite "drugstore scene" in Act Two). The resultant entities are both honest and profound.

In closing, it should be noted that the critics have been wrong before, and so has the popular audience. Each play must stand on its own merits. *Our Town* is a work which cannot be ignored merely because it is popular. The final condemnation of this play by those who do not approve of it has been that it is inconsistent, that the first two acts are comic and the third is tragic. This is in a sense true; and obviously in contradiction of Aristotelian principles. However, life is both "the human comedy" and "the incredible fate" of man. There is joy mingled everlastingly with despair. In his sanest moments, man is aware of how fleeting both the joy and the despair are. He knows that the end of the human comedy is the awakening into "the undiscover'd country from whose bourn no traveler returns."

As *Our Town* quite brilliantly shows, life is a paradox, and so it is not amazing that man paradoxically retains his faith that in death, too, there is life and a greater consciousness. Like Oedipus before her, Emily finds a place in dramatic literature as a tragic figure of enormous dimensions, for in her blindness, or death, she gains the true ability really to see and understand.

Our Town as a Failed Tragedy

George D. Stephens

George D. Stephens challenges Arthur Ballet's claim
that *Our Town* is a great American tragedy and that
Emily is a tragic figure. Stephens argues that Emily,
unlike a tragic figure such as Shakespeare's Hamlet, is
not a fully realized personality. In Wilder's expressionistic play, Emily is a type more than an individual;
hence, the audience never feels emotionally involved
with her. Emily does not struggle, things happen to
her; she is pathetic, not tragic; and her discoveries
among the dead are not particularly profound or elevating. Stephens also reasons that Grover's Corners is
a setting of romantic optimism; it does not reveal a
stern world where a tragic figure must endure the
capriciousness of fate, guilt, weakness, and deep-
seated pain before coming to a meaningful understanding of life and self. Stephens concludes that *Our
Town* is popular because it is *not* tragic. Instead, its
popularity rests on the fact that it is charming, folksy,
and nostalgic.

George Stephens is a professor of English at Long
Beach State College in Long Beach, California. He has
contributed numerous critical articles to periodicals
like the *Southwest Review* and the *Educational Forum.*

In our longing for an unattainable perfection, perhaps it is to
be expected that the attempt to find "the great American
novel" and "the great American drama" should continue.
But ours is a nation of great size and remarkable variety; it
poses a complex problem for the writer who attempts to syn-
thesize and interpret its life for us. Though this is doubtful,
considering the nature of art and our subjective reaction to
it, in time a work may appear which will by overwhelming

Reprinted from George D. Stephens, *"Our Town:* Great American Tragedy?" *Modern
Drama,* February 1959, pp. 258–64, by permission of *Modern Drama.*

weight of opinion be awarded the title of "the greatest."
Meanwhile, this search sometimes leads to extravagant
claims.

Such a claim, which seems unwarranted in view of the
limits of the play set by the author, has been made for
Thornton Wilder's *Our Town*. Professor Arthur H. Ballet,
writing in *The English Journal* of May, 1956, finds in *Our
Town* "the great American drama." This judgment seems to
have been encouraged by the continuing popularity of the
play as evidenced in performances, mainly in college and
community theatres, and by discussion in critical and academic circles. Cited also is the choice of Wilder as their "favorite living playwright" by a group of American dramatists
polled in *The Saturday Review*.

It is not my purpose to denigrate *Our Town*, which is,
within the limits of its subject, form, and point of view, an
interesting and valuable play. But one must challenge the
claim that it is the greatest American play; that it is an out-
standing tragedy; and that Emily is "a tragic figure of enormous dimensions." Necessarily this discussion will have to
take the form, in part, of an examination of Professor Ballet's
article.

According to his analysis, *Our Town* is like classic tragedy
in several respects. Structurally it is a trilogy, with each act
serving as a separate play; Act Three expands "the first parts
of the trilogy into a complex of eternity where the mystery of
life is culminated in death. Like its Greek predecessors, *Our
Town* is concerned with the great and continuing cycle of
life . . . man's closest understanding of eternity, his finest
artistic expression of what he senses to be a mission and a
purpose. The trilogy, thus considered, admirably reinter-
prets this concept in modern terms and language and form,
finding its roots in what is probably the finest drama of all
time: Sophocles' *Oedipus Rex*." The Stage Manager, who
serves as chorus, is further evidence of affinity with classic
drama: "[He] represents the observing community . . . his serious but twinkling control of the progress of the play [pre-
vents] over-identification, which would destroy the higher
implications. . . ." There is, also, a classic simplicity in the
setting. "Returning to a theatrical tradition ranging from
Athens to Elizabethan England, [the play] returns . . . to a
plane of imagination rather than realistic reproduction and
soars above mundane distractions of actuality. . . ."

At first glance, in this interpretation, *Our Town* falls short of accomplishing the purgation and ennoblement called for by Aristotle as essential effects of tragedy; but further analysis shows that death "is the fear-agent employed as a catharsis," and Emily, "the smallest of God's creatures, a young mother who becomes aware of the tragedy of life," is ennobled by death "to understand how wonderful life is. . . ." Further, Wilder establishes Grover's Corners as a part of the cosmos, thus pointing the way to "a higher level of understanding" of the rôle played by man. In accord with Aristotelian standards, therefore, the play is "elevating" and "approaches significance as a tragedy."

Admittedly the play is sentimental. Frank M. Whiting (*An Introduction to the Theatre*) is quoted: "It [*Our Town*] is an honest and revealing portrait of small-town American life. It has been criticized as sentimental, but American life is sentimental; Emily, George, and the others give us a far more genuine insight into twentieth-century American living than do the studies of neurotics, gangsters and the sexually frustrated." However, Professor Ballet believes this sentimentality is "without sententiousness; [the play] has romance without romanticism, and innocence without naïvete." Finally, although the criticism that the first two acts are comic and the third tragic is "in a sense true, and obviously in contradiction of Aristotelian principles . . . Life is both 'the human comedy' and 'the incredible fate' of man." And the conclusion is: "As *Our Town* quite brilliantly shows, life is a paradox, and so it is not amazing that man paradoxically retains his faith that in death, too, there is life and a great consciousness. Like Oedipus before her, Emily finds a place in dramatic literature as a tragic figure of enormous dimensions, for in her blindness, or death, she gains the true ability to see and understand."

The foregoing, I hope, represents the essential aspects of the article. In summarizing, probably I have done it less than justice, but I have tried to give it as accurately as possible in this abridged form.

THE MOTIVATING IDEA OF EACH ACT

It is questionable whether *Our Town* can be called tragedy at all in any worthy definition of the term. Surely it does not fit Aristotelian standards; or, to put it another way, it is not like Greek tragedy. The three acts are like the separate plays of

Aeschylus' *Oresteia* in not much more than that Wilder divided his play into three acts and gave each a theme or motivating idea. Consider the *Oresteia*: each play, while essential to the great whole, is complete within itself, with carefully built up situation and plot, characterization in variety and depth, and conflict leading to a solution. Imaginatively we participate in and are moved by the power and beauty of *Agamemnon* and the other plays because in each Aeschylus has created the details of a complete story.

Act One of *Our Town*, illustrating or symbolizing The Daily Life of Grover's Corners, could not possibly stand alone as a complete play, nor could the other acts. More than a third of Act One, in fact, is comment of a sociological or historical nature. Through the Stage Manager, who acts as both commentator and participant—and as such he has a function similar to that of the Greek chorus—and others, we are given selected information about this small New Hampshire town as it was in the early part of the twentieth century. (Incidentally, the Stage Manager and the scenery, or lack of it, are reminiscent of the Chinese theatre, with which Wilder is known to be familiar.) Employing short, episodic scenes, Wilder focuses on two middle-class families, the Webbs and the Gibbs, who are evidently meant to be typical of such small-town American people. His emphasis is on social relationships rather than on individual character, on the town rather than on Mrs. Gibbs or George or Emily.

Act Two, entitled Love and Marriage, carries on the story of the town by giving further information and, more important, by concentrating on the two young people who create a family and thus insure the town's continued existence. Wilder establishes a somewhat deeper emotional involvement with his characters than in Act One by his skillful description of love, courtship, and marriage, but again George and Emily are not sharply and deeply individualized. They are, and are meant to be, symbols of youth; they are abstractions or forces clothed in words. "People were made to live two-by-two," says the Stage Manager, emphasizing the social relationship.

Act Three, extending the story through death into eternity and so raising it to a universal plane, is the principal basis for the claims made for the play as significant tragedy. In death Emily discovers, as have the other dead, that the living are troubled and blind, and that life is short and sad. In considerable part Wilder focuses on Emily to illustrate these truths, but again her character, as an individual, fails to acquire depth. She is still only one of the group who are given much attention and who, all of them together, living and dead, symbolize the persistence of human life as it exists in the community. The cycle of life persists, the life of the town, a small but significant part of mysterious eternity. In short, Emily is not the protagonist of the play; the protagonist is the town itself.

THE PLAY'S EXPRESSIONISM

The expressionist form chosen for the play is well adapted to the author's purposes. In "The Family in Modern Drama" (*The Atlantic Monthly*, April, 1956), Arthur Miller suggests that realism is the best medium for presentation of "the primarily familial relation," expressionism for "the primarily social relation." He cites *Our Town* as an example of the latter. While I can think of dramatists who use expressionism successfully to interpret individual and family relationships (Strindberg, Pirandello, O'Neill, for instance, and to a certain extent Miller himself in *Death of a Salesman*), I agree that expressionism is well adapted to emphasize social ideas or forces. More obviously symbolic than realism, more "theatrical" in that it does not seek primarily to produce an illusion of reality, expressionism forces the audience into a more intellectual or objective attitude.

However, such objectivity does not, I believe, provide a strong medium for tragedy. While he is involved in society, the individual must be the hero and the victim of tragedy. Oedipus and Hamlet and Lear are in part symbolic, but more important, they are multi-dimensional, fully realized personalities. They "come alive," as they must do to provide the emotional involvement necessary for the tragic reaction. I am aware of the presentational or symbolic quality in Greek tragedy; in a sense, the technique was similar to that of modern expressionism. We, of course, cannot know just what the reaction of the Greek audience was, but it must have been conscious of the actors as larger than life-size, as symbolic figures. At the same time, I cannot believe that it did not also participate in the fortunes of the tragic characters as representatives of living people; it must have recognized universal human qualities in them, rejoiced and suffered with them. Else why should Aristotle name terror and pity as productive of catharsis? The last plays of Aeschylus, and certainly the plays of Sophocles and Euripides, were, as all tragedy must be, basically realistic. From story, from what happens to the characters, comes meaning, come terror and pity and beauty. And what stories the Greeks told!

EMILY AS A PATHETIC FIGURE

Through the continual intervention of the Stage Manager, Wilder never allows his audience to forget that it is witnessing a symbolic presentation. But no one can feel about a town as he does about a person. Insofar as he focuses on his people, Wilder involves his audience with them emotionally as well as intellectually; but it is not a strong, complex involvement. Emily is simple and superficial; she typifies the sweet, innocent girl who progresses normally through adolescent awakening into courtship, marriage, and early death in childbirth. The sketchiest comparison with Oedipus, Electra, Medea, Hamlet, Lear, or for that matter Willy Loman of *Death of a Salesman,* Blanche of *A Streetcar Named Desire,* or Mio of *Winterset,* shows how far she falls short. The tragic protagonist, fully realized as an individual, is involved from beginning to end in an impossible struggle with fate, circumstance, or society, with his antagonists, himself, and death—doomed to failure but perhaps finding or projecting, after immense suffering, a kind of reconciliation or enlightenment. To him, what must be, cannot be; what cannot be, must be. Emily does not struggle; things merely happen to her. Her fate is the common one, and it evokes a gentle sadness. She is pathetic, not tragic.

Is Emily ennobled, and the audience or reader "elevated," by her understanding of "how wonderful life is"? What she as a character understands mainly, it seems to me, and this only after death, is that the living are ignorant and troubled and that life is short and sad. She is made to say, "Oh, earth, you're too wonderful for anybody to realize you. Do any human beings ever realize life while they live it?" Perhaps this is true, but it is hardly either profound or elevating. (Indeed, one might suppose that there are people who understand, while still living, something about the nature of life: evidently Wilder himself does.) True, in the play as a whole Wilder apparently wishes to illustrate the paradoxical nature of life: persistent and wonderful as well as short and troubled. But again, the context chosen, and therefore the effect produced, is not that of tragedy; it is, rather, that of gentle nostalgia or, to put it another way, sentimental romanticism.

GROVER'S CORNERS AS A ROMANTIC SETTING

The assertion that *Our Town* is of the romantic genre is defensible on several counts. One notes that Wilder chooses fantasy in Act Three to convey the full measure of his meaning, basing his presentation on the romantic assumption that there is an existence after death. What other play highly regarded as tragic, of the past or contemporary, calls on such fantasy? Tragedy shows the agonies of its people in this life, draws its meaning and its catharsis from experience in the here and now.

Further, the picture of small town or village life—again, *Our Town*'s theme and chief preoccupation—owes much to the nineteenth-century American sentimental myth of the beautiful people of the beautiful village, a myth scotched once for all, one would have thought, by the likes of Edgar Watson Howe, Harold Frederic, Edgar Lee Masters, Sinclair Lewis, Sherwood Anderson, William Faulkner. Significantly, Wilder chooses the pre-World War I decade for his time, a simpler, more peaceful era, one that can be seen by an American audience through a nostalgic haze evoked by memories (or illusions) of "the good old days in the old home town." The pic-

---

WILDER'S OPTIMISM

In an October 15, 1973 Los Angeles Times *article entitled "Thornton Wilder on Life Today," journalist Robert J. Donovan quotes Thornton Wilder's simple optimism.*

"In a nutshell, . . . this is an age of transition.

"An age of transition is difficult for everybody—difficult for parents, difficult for children, difficult for you in the journalistic world. But it is an exciting age. Something is straining to be born."

If this is cause for pessimism, it has been lost on the author of such works as *Our Town, The Skin of Our Teeth* and *The Bridge of San Luis Rey* and the friend of F. Scott Fitzgerald, Ernest Hemingway and Gertrude Stein.

"I am of an optimistic nature—a grasshopper," he said in an interview the other day. "I enjoy hoppiting around. I'm happy every day. I don't view with alarm every day. Having lived so long, I have seen many things. All history has been troubled, but when you are in the kind of transition we are in now, the trouble is more apparent than at other times."

ture of Grover's Corners and its people is highly selective: omitted are mean, sordid, cruel, generally unpleasant details. These are wholesome, pleasant, average or normal, "good" people; and wholesome, pleasant, average or normal, "good" things (including death) happen to them. It is, as Emily says, "a very nice town"—too nice, from a rational and realistic point of view. There are, as Frank Whiting points out, no neurotics, gangsters, or sexually frustrated people; deleted, in fact, are sex (except the romantic variety), violence, cruelty, poverty. Even the town problem, Simon Stimson, who comes drunk to direct choir practice and finally (we are told, not shown) kills himself, is treated with admirable (and therefore sentimental because it is unconvincing) understanding and tolerance by his fellow citizens.

What we have here, then, is substitution of secluded garden for world. (In contrast, Shakespeare has Mercutio outside the garden cracking bawdy jokes about girls at the same time that Romeo and Juliet are making ecstatic love.) It is true that Wilder takes pains to establish Grover's Corners as part of the universe, or "the mind of God," as he puts it. The town, he seems to be saying, is integral with a process which is permanent, orderly, and good. Assuredly the play is a statement of faith in man. During the wedding the Stage Manager stops the action to comment on the eternity of which man is part: "And don't forget the other witnesses at the wedding—the ancestors. Millions of them." He also says, ". . . every child born into the world is nature's attempt to make a perfect human being."

This is the view of romantic naturalism: with Newtonian and Cartesian rationalism as distant base, strained through the idealistic sensibilities of Rousseau, Kant, Wordsworth, Carlyle, Emerson, Whitman, and sentimentalized by the Victorians. It recalls the lines from *Pippa Passes*, "God's in his heaven,/All's right with the world!"—which did not represent Browning's feeling but which have come to stand for the smug optimism of some of his middle-class contemporaries. By suggesting this idea, *Our Town* acquires depth and dimension; but it is not thereby raised to the status of tragedy. The universe includes Grover's Corners, but Grover's Corners does not include the universe. That is to say, the reading of life here is heavily weighted with sentimental optimism; *Our Town* ignores a complex of knowledge revealed to us through experience, reason, and science.

The affirmations of tragedy, its statement of faith in man's strength and courage, are not like the bland assurance of this play. Tragedy is stern, beyond tears. Man endures in spite of capricious, incredible and unendurable fate or circumstance; in spite of guilt and weakness; in spite of enormous, soul-shattering pain. In his dilemma the tragic protagonist understands little or nothing about the forces which are destroying him—until, perhaps, a glimmer of light appears as he faces death; yet he is defiant or at least stoical. Esdras' speech at the end of Maxwell Anderson's *Winterset* has the spirit of tragedy:

> . . . this is the glory of earth-born men and women, not to cringe, never to yield, but standing, take defeat implacable and defiant, die unsubmitting. . . .

> . . . in this hard star-adventure, knowing not what the fires mean to right and left, nor whether a meaning was intended or presumed, man can stand up, and look out blind, and say: in all these turning lights I find no clue, only a masterless night, and in my blood no certain answer, yet is my mind my own, yet is my heart a cry toward something dim in distance, which is higher than I am and makes me emperor of the endless dark even in seeking!

In questioning the claim that *Our Town* is tragedy of a high order I do not, as I have said, wish to deny that it has considerable interest and value. Certainly it has been popular. Professor Ballet is worried that it may be ignored merely because it *is* popular, and he is concerned to account for the popularity, for the "tragic complexities" of the play do not explain its affectionate appeal. This, he believes, rests on the picture of familiar daily life, showing "the homely verities of human existence." He implies, though he does not directly say so, that the play gives us an idealized version of life: "If *Our Town* does not reflect life as it really is, at least it suggests what the daily life should be like, and the audience approves."

THE POPULARITY OF THE PLAY

This is perceptive: *Our Town* is popular, in part at least, because it is not tragic. The American public has approved of it because of its charming, folksy presentation of simple, "good" people, its sentimentally idealized account of the small town. It projects a vision of a time and place which have vanished from the American scene, which never existed in fact—not just as shown in the play, at any rate—but which some people believe or like to think existed. So they view this symbolic picture of Grover's Corners through a mist of gentle, romantic nostalgia. Further, the optimistic assurance that this town has an enduring place in an orderly, meaningful universe, plus the statement of faith in man, carries strong appeal. In addition, the "truths" about life discovered by Emily and the others—that the living are blind, troubled, etc., are just such observations as would impress the average audience. Emily's pathetic death, popularly mistaken for tragedy, is evocative of tender feelings of pity. And finally, the expressionist technique, unusual or unfamiliar to many, adds an extra fillip of interest. It is not difficult to account for the play's popularity.

Within the limits of its purpose, subject, and form, certainly *Our Town* is a valuable contribution to the drama and culture of the United States. It is indeed worthy of respect and praise. However, I do not believe it is at present established as the greatest American play, and certainly it is not, in my opinion, a play which ranks with the great tragedies—not, in fact, a tragedy at all.

In his engaging article, "A Platform and a Passion or Two" (*Harper's Magazine*, October, 1957), Mr. Wilder writes: "And as I view the work of my contemporaries I seem to feel that I am exceptional in one thing—I give (don't I?) the impression of having enormously enjoyed it [life]?" Yes, but this is not, is it, the mental climate which produces a writer of tragedy?

CHAPTER 2

Themes and Characterization in *Our Town*

READINGS ON
OUR TOWN

Characters in *Our Town*

Jan Austell

Jan Austell contends that the essential character
traits and behavior of the characters in *Our Town* are
static. The dominant figure in *Our Town*, the Stage
Manager, is sincere, fascinated by facts, easygoing,
straightforward, and, at times, whimsical. Serving as
the link between the players and the audience, the
Stage Manager has the godlike ability to step back
and forth in time and in and out of the characters.
Despite his casual demeanor, he reveals fundamental truths about life and human beings.

 In addition, Austell argues that the two major families in the play, the Gibbses and the Webbs, are fundamentally the same; both are admired, both contribute to the community, and both experience loss.
According to Austell, the families embody the theme
that humans share common experiences as well as
human similarities in beliefs, values, moral standards, vulnerabilities, and irritations. The children
in both families are also typical, representing youths
who must mature. Austell writes that the minor
characters are essentially ordinary; each revealing at
least one basic and distinct human trait.

 In addition to *What's in a Play*, Jan Austell has
written numerous theatrical articles and play reviews.

Before we discuss the individual characters in *Our Town* to
determine what each actor should try to accomplish in his
role, let us consider the extent to which Wilder has developed
them. Each one, with the possible exception of Mrs. Gibbs,
has essentially the same personality, demeanor, or nature at
the end of the play that he had at the beginning. None of them
changes from good to bad, from gentle and kind to hard-bitten
and selfish, or even from shy to brash. To be sure, some of the
characters learn certain things during the play—George

learns that some people think he is stuck-up and his mother, Mrs. Gibbs, acquires in death the knowledge that most people waste the precious minutes of their lives. Emily learns the same lesson from her. Also, during the play, the stage manager seems to become increasingly thoughtful and knowing, but the characters themselves do not *change* in their essential behavior. Throughout the play they keep the same personality traits that they display on making their first appearance. What sort of actors are needed to portray these characters? What should a director consider in casting the parts?

THE STAGE MANAGER

Wilder states in his directions that when the stage manager appears before the house lights go down and arranges a few pieces of furniture on stage, he should be wearing a hat and he should have a pipe, which he may be smoking although Wilder does not require him to do so. He should be calm and casual as he watches late members of the audience take their seats. Wilder gives no specific indication of the stage manager's age or his physical size, but on the basis of his opening speech we know that the stage manager should be a straightforward, pleasant man, relaxed and happy about having a group of people to whom he can introduce Grover's Corners and the people who live there. He has none of the traits of the hard-selling salesman trying to convince a customer he should buy something. On the contrary, because he is neither condescending nor overexuberant, he has the quality of a man who has been asked to guide some willing visitors through a place he knows and loves and for whom every detail has a cherished value. He almost seems to say to them, "If you keep your eyes and ears open, you will learn more than you thought you would." And he is entirely sincere in this attitude; he is not trying to fool or bully anyone.

The stage manager is a man who appreciates facts and who thinks his visitors will too. He notes the longitude and latitude of the town, indicates where the churches are, and reports what grows in Mrs. Gibbs' garden. But his speeches also show that he has a certain whimsy and a rather dry sense of humor. After telling several facts about the town and the play, the stage manager muses on the morning star for a moment before showing how the town is laid out. The brightness of the star—a little thing—is just as important to this perceptive man as the other details. He makes wry remarks about the "scenery for those who think they have to have scenery"; about the similarity between Mrs. Webb's and Mrs. Gibbs' gardens; about the town people who sleep late—later than 5:45 A.M.; and about the young people who, after passing their last examinations in solid geometry and Cicero's Orations, "suddenly feel themselves fit to be married." None of these remarks is barbed with derision or spoken with anything but amused acceptance or fond acknowledgment.

The stage manager is the audience's link with life in Grover's Corners; as he "manages" the action of the play, he is both something more than one of the townspeople and something more than one of the audience. Although he is anywhere from 35 to 65 years old, he seems ageless. The man is not God, but he seems to have the God-like ability to step back and forth in time, in and out of the lives of the characters, and, in Act III, from human life on earth to an existence after death—all in order to show members of the audience everything he thinks they should know about "our" town.

As *Our Town* begins, the audience has no idea who the stage manager is or what his function will be. Because he appears to be simply an average fellow with a pleasing manner about him, the stage manager is rather like the town itself: attractive enough in its own way, but hardly spectacular. Yet both the stage manager and the town show, gradually and simply, some fundamental truths about ourselves and about human life.

While the part of the stage manager is probably the most difficult one in the play, it does not necessarily follow that the role must be taken by the most popular or noteworthy actor available. A talented but unfamiliar professional or an amateur actor will stand a better chance of communicating the ideas and the atmosphere that Wilder wanted to present than will a well-known actor. If the audience recognizes the actor portraying the stage manager, it will immediately cloak him with preconceived notions. Only when it can put aside these notions will the audience believe in the actor's portrayal. It is essential to the play that the stage manager be seen and heard *first* as a nondescript, affable person, willing to guide other people if they want to be guided, and only *later* as a man unique in his wisdom and understanding, entirely in control of the action that takes place.

THE GIBBSES AND THE WEBBS

With the help of the stage manager, Wilder focuses the attention of the audience on two families in Grover's Corners:

the Gibbses and the Webbs. In considering actors to play these characters, the director is faced with a special problem, which grows out of the paradox at the heart of the play. These two families are superficially different; yet, they are essentially similar.

George Gibbs has a younger sister and Emily Webb has a younger brother, but the point is that both families have children. George is a good baseball player and Emily is a bright student, but the point is that they both have certain abilities which, while George and Emily are young, are admired by others. Doc Gibbs is interested in the Civil War and knows much of its history; Editor Webb is interested in Napoleon's career, but the point is that both men in their enjoyment of particular phases of history have hobbies or avocations. Editor Webb is recognized as the authority on Grover's Corners' vital statistics, while the hospital is named after Doc Gibbs, but the point is that both men know the town well and make significant contributions to the community. Mrs. Gibbs dies of pneumonia during a visit to her daughter's home in Ohio and young Wally Webb dies when his appendix bursts on a Boy Scout trip to Crawford Notch, but the point is that each family suffers the unexpected and great loss of one of its members. Wilder is, of course, specifically presenting the Gibbs family and the Webb family and portions of their lives, but since a primary assumption in *Our Town* is that human beings share the common experience of life, the Gibbses and the Webbs represent not differences among human beings but fundamental similarities.

It would be a mistake for a director and his actors to invent or overemphasize any particular traits they see in the individual parts, just as it would be a mistake to strive to make Wilder's characters absolutely identical. Since the two couples, Doc and Mrs. Gibbs and Editor and Mrs. Webb, are so similar, the temptation is strong for an actor to intensify some distinctive aspect of the character he is playing. The error would be obvious if an actress took Mrs. Webb's remark, "I'd rather have my children healthy than bright," as a key to the character of Mrs. Webb and then proceeded to portray her as an anti-intellectual health fanatic. Similarly, simply because Mrs. Gibbs says that ever since she has been a little girl she has wanted to see Paris, France, and that before dying everyone "ought to see a country where they don't talk and think in English and don't even want to," there is no justification for portraying Mrs. Gibbs as a dreamer who is unhappy in her marriage and is dissatisfied with her life. The opposite temptation is just as insidious. If a director required Editor and Mrs. Webb to duplicate the gestures, mannerisms, and dress of Doc and Mrs. Gibbs, he would make it difficult for the audience to identify sympathetically with the characters because they would seem to be satirizing or poking fun at themselves and the audience.

THE GIBBSES AND WEBBS AS AVERAGE AMERICAN FAMILIES

The Gibbses and the Webbs are neither abnormal extremist types, nor faceless nonentities; they are sincere, average people. Naturally, they have their idiosyncrasies. Doc Gibbs likes to ramble over the Gettysburg battlefield, Editor Webb is interested in incubators for chickens. Mrs. Gibbs enjoys making plans for a trip, and Mrs. Webb yearns to can forty quarts of beans. But also they have the same basic beliefs, habits, and standards of right and wrong, the same willingness to be cheerful, amusing, and tolerant, and the same vulnerability to nervousness and irritation that all people have. They are not exaggerated and therefore false versions of average people; they are the people themselves: the genuine articles.

To demonstrate authenticity, similarity, and variety at the same time is not easy. Fortunately, because it is constructed in a series of short scenes or moments, Wilder's script gives the actors a number of opportunities to be distinct as individuals while retaining the common bonds of human life. Doc Gibbs doubtless knows Grover's Corners pretty well, but it is Editor Webb who is given the job of explaining particular features of the town to the audience. It would be surprising if Editor and Mrs. Webb were above arguing, but it is Doc Gibbs and his wife who fuss about the gossip over Simon Stimson, about vacations, and about the town being citified by people who lock their doors. It is likely that the Webb children are irresponsible at times, but it is Doc Gibbs who has a talk with George about working around the house to help his mother. Doc and Mrs. Gibbs doubtless talk with George about married life, but not on stage; Wilder assigns such a conversation to George and Editor Webb.

The best generalization to use in choosing actors to play the Gibbses and the Webbs, as well as the rest of the characters in *Our Town*, is to keep them physically different from each other. The Gibbs family might be shorter and heavier than the Webbs. Editor Webb might wear eyeglasses whereas Doc Gibbs would not. Mrs. Webb might have blond hair whereas Mrs. Gibbs would have dark brown hair, and so on. Such diversity of physical appearance among the actors has its justification in Wilder's point that there is constant variety in life and that it is worth treasuring.

THE CHILDREN

The children in these two families, George and Emily, Rebecca and Wally, must be accepted by the audience as being typical just as their parents are. Wilder has made it somewhat easier, though, for the youngsters to be distinct in their roles than he has for their stage parents. George Gibbs does not have a counterpart in the Webb family as does his father Doc Gibbs in the person of Editor Webb. Emily Webb is the only girl her age in the play while her mother is virtually the same as George's mother. Still younger, Rebecca and Wally are to look, sound, and act like a "kid sister" and a "kid brother." They are not counterparts of each other, and since they are younger, they do not compete with George and Emily as counterparts. Rebecca likes dresses, money, and attention; Wally likes to read and to collect stamps. Their task is to represent youth but they have less to do in *Our Town* than George and Emily. During the play, George and Emily must grow up. The audience will believe they are doing so if the actors playing their parts clearly show each step in the process. The characters of George and Emily do not change but they are revealed slowly as they mature, trait by trait, scene by scene. Wilder's script is particularly helpful because each scene in which either George or Emily appears emphasizes one of their traits or characteristics. In one scene we see George's self-centered concern about his school work and baseball; in another, his being ashamed of himself for shirking responsibility, and in another, his rather awkward gallantry with Emily. We see Emily's preoccupation with being pretty in one scene; in another, her shyness with George; in another, her affection for him. These changes in emphasis represent the maturing process.

THE OTHER TOWNSPEOPLE

Just as the major characters in the play are not a special breed of spectacular individuals, neither are the minor ones. An audience can readily believe in the entirely ordinary and, to some, familiar figures of the newspaper boys, Joe Crowell, Jr. and his brother Si, and the milkman, Howie Newsome. While amusing, it is not extraordinary or unusual that Joe is sorry to see his schoolteacher getting married; that Si hates to have George give up baseball just to get married; or that Howie's horse is old and eccentric and that his milk separator acts up occasionally. Not everyone knows a university professor, but anyone in an audience has probably met a person like Professor Willard with a scholarly bearing who knows one subject well and who has a tendency to be somewhat long-winded and disorganized. A woman like Mrs. Soames, who loves gossip and who busies herself enthusiastically with all the things that are going on around her, is not unusual. Nor is a man like Simon Stimson, the one sour character in the play. He seems to feel constantly let down by life and by people, perhaps because he is a perfectionist. The other minor characters, including those at the wedding, those in the graveyard, and those in the audience who address questions to Editor Webb, are all recognizable. They are not as fully developed as the stage manager and the members of the Gibbs and Webb families, but each reveals in his lines at least one distinct human trait for an actor to use in his portrayal.

Universality in
Our Town

Malcolm Goldstein

Despite the early doubts of its director, Ted Harris, *Our Town* connected immediately with its Broadway audience, ultimately generating profits, awards, prestige, and a loyal following both in the United States and abroad. Malcolm Goldstein suggests that Wilder drew heavily on elements from earlier plays to construct *Our Town:* the lack of scenery, the use of a stage manager, delivery devices, and details of dialogue.

Goldstein writes that the setting, the main characters, and the play's events are universal. The setting, Grover's Corners, is on the one hand very unremarkable, just another spot on the globe, but on the other hand represents all places because what happens there, in general terms, happens in the lives of all people. Goldstein argues that the main characters, George Gibbs and Emily Webb, reflect a larger, universal pattern of human adventure. Their joys and their sorrows represent the emotions shared by all people, the sum of human passions. Additionally, Goldstein reasons that the common, everyday events of the play reflect Wilder's universal theme that the cause of one's unhappiness is not the failure to achieve greatness, but the failure to understand and appreciate the importance of ordinary existence.

Malcolm Goldstein has written widely on the theater and drama. He is the author of *The Political Stage: American Drama and Theater of the Great Depression.*

Wilder was no stranger to the New York theater before the opening of *Our Town.* His prior record had included three productions: the off-Broadway presentation of his *The Trumpet Shall Sound* in 1926, the unsuccessful Broadway showing of André Obey's *Lucrece* in 1932 in his translation, and Jed Harris's highly praised staging of his translation of Ibsen's *A Doll's House* in 1937, also on Broadway. The list is not extensive, but together the three experiences offered a hint of what was to come with a major Broadway production of a piece entirely his own.

For the second time he worked with Harris, a thoroughly trained man of the theater whose abundant charm often gave way before an iron determination to secure the production values which would insure a run. As was typical of him, he drove and quarreled with Wilder during rehearsals, but, after a difficult tryout period, proved the soundness of his judgment with a successful production. A few preliminary performances given in Princeton went very well and seemed to augur good fortune, but in Boston, where it was scheduled for two weeks, the play was roundly damned. Since the Boston audience is no more discriminating than the Princeton or New York audience despite the traditional claim of every city that it is the most difficult to please, the future of *Our Town* was beyond prediction in the last days before the opening. Harris therefore decided to cut his losses and bring in the play one week ahead of schedule. To do so, it was necessary for him to make an interim booking of a temporarily vacant house for *one night only*, February 4, 1938, after which, if all went well, he would lease another theater for the run of the play.

OUR TOWN'S SUCCESS

The result was what Harris had hoped: the play caught on at once, ran through the season and into November of the next, and won a second Pulitzer Prize for Wilder. Since the end of the Broadway run it has been produced almost nightly in community and college theaters across America, with a financial reward to the author of $400,000 as of the end of 1963. It has been filmed (with most of the cast of the Broadway production) and has been televised twice, the second time in a musical version. Although Harris has been eager to say that it lost money for him in San Francisco and Los Angeles as well as in Boston, the New England metropolis is in fact the only American city to have withheld approval. Abroad also, as *Unsere Kleine Stadt* or *Notre petite ville*, it has held the stage, although at its London debut in 1946, again under Harris's direction, the play did not take. At the time of the present writing *Our Town* has earned a position as a classic more secure than has been accorded any other work in the American repertory, the international reputation of Eugene O'Neill notwithstanding.

WILDER'S GROWTH AS A WRITER

At the beginning of the 1930's Wilder planted the seed which was to give growth to this remarkably successful play. The sceneryless one-acts of 1931 are the source of its form, of the employment of the Stage Manager-*conférencier*, of certain details of dialogue, and of the name of the town, Grover's Corners, where the action unfolds. From *Pullman Car Hiawatha* comes the notion of presenting the historical and sociological background, a device of importance to the expression of theme in both works, and from the same play comes the young heroine's heartfelt series of farewells to remembered scenes of happiness at the time of her death. From *The Long Christmas Dinner* come her touching but overdue words of praise for her mother. The central material of the third act, the heroine's return to life for a repetition of one day of childhood, has, it will be remembered, an earlier source in *The Woman of Andros*. In borrowing from his own writing for works of ever-broadening scope, Wilder had revealed his capacity for growth with each new publication since *The Cabala*. Yet in no work before *Our Town* had he shown such an amazing spring forward. . . .

THE UNIVERSALITY OF GROVER'S CORNERS

Although the play begins and ends in one precisely described place, Grover's Corners, New Hampshire, it ranges far beyond the village boundaries in each of its three acts. By eliminating scenery and props, except for two small trellises to appease persons who cannot do without scenery, Wilder avoids from the outset any suggestion that the *meaning* of the action relates only to Grover's Corners, and yet, through the dialogue and the expository remarks of the Stage Manager, he retains enough of the New England flavor to remind the audience of the starting point, so to speak, of the nation in which it lives. He begins, then, in the small New England town and from it moves out to embrace all creation. The timespan of the play runs from 1901 to 1913, a period recent enough in 1938 to appeal to the memory of the audience, but still distant enough to be free of restrictive contemporary associations.

The plot is the story of two neighboring households, the Gibbs and Webb families Their lives are in no way sensational or special; nothing has happened to them that might set them off either as heroes or as victims. True, the family heads are professional men—*Dr.* Gibbs and *Editor* Webb—but the distinction implied in the titles serves only to confer upon them a degree of familiarity with human problems, and this they are able to communicate to the audience. As one device out of many to link Grover's Corners to the great world beyond, Wilder also gives the two men distinctive hobbies. Dr. Gibbs devotes all his spare time to studies of the Civil War, and Editor Webb is equally fascinated by the life of Napoleon. Like its principal families, the town itself, considered as a place on the map, possesses a distinguishing but unastonishing "background," as described by local authorities: so many members of each religious denomination live in it, the ground under it was founded in such-and-such geological eras, the birth and death rates are thus and so. The purpose of this quite ordinary information is not to particularize the town; rather, it serves to underline the fact that Grover's Corners, the home of the Gibbses and the Webbs, is just another spot in the cosmos. But at the same time that it is a place of no importance, the town represents the universe, and whatever occurs to its inhabitants is an expression, in very general terms, of the chief events in the lives of all people.

The scenes devised by Wilder are moments of eternity singled out for our attention and played against the panorama of infinity. The first act is titled "The Daily Life," and offers such details as the early-morning milk delivery, the family breakfast, and the children's departure for school. Proceeding from dawn till bedtime, at every turn the action distills poignance from the commonplace, including even so unremarkable an occurrence as the children's struggle with homework. In choosing this title for the act, Wilder would seem for the moment to ignore the remarks of Gertrude Stein, who said that the Americans have no daily life in the sense that the English have one—that is, that we do not think as a nation in terms of a simple, unchanging routine. But the phrase and the routine activities covered by it are useful to Wilder insofar as they carry the notion that these New Englanders, engaged as they are in ordinary, mundane duties, are authentic representatives of the entire race. Similarly, the titles of the second and third acts, "Love and Marriage" and "Death," the latter only hinted at, not explicitly given, describe the fundamental material of existence.

THE UNIVERSALITY OF THE CHARACTERS

Of the twenty-two characters who pass across the stage, most are present only to populate the arena whose principal actors are George Gibbs and Emily Webb, the older children of the two families Through the conduct of their lives, which, as we see them on Wilder's bare stage, they lead in infinite space at a point in the endless continuum of time, emerges in little the general pattern of the human adven-

---

WILDER'S PREOCCUPATION WITH THE VASTNESS OF HISTORY
In a 1956 interview with Richard H. Goldstone for the Paris Review, *reprinted in* Conversations With Thornton Wilder, *Wilder discusses the impact of one central theme in his work: the overwhelming gulf between the particulars of everyday life and the vast stretch of historical time.*

INTERVIEWER: Someone has said—one of your dramatist colleagues, I believe, I can't remember which one—that a writer deals with only one or two ideas throughout his work. Would you say your work reflects those one or two ideas?

WILDER: Yes, I think so. I have become aware of it myself only recently. Those ideas seem to have prompted my work before I realized it. Now, at my age, I am amused by the circumstance that what is now conscious with me was for a long time latent. One of those ideas is this: an unresting preoccupation with the surprise of the gulf between each tiny occasion of the daily life and the vast stretches of time and place in which every individual plays his role. By that I mean the absurdity of any single person's claim to the importance of his saying, "I love!" "I suffer!" when one thinks of the background of the billions who have lived and died, who are living and dying, and presumably will live and die.

This was particularly developed in me by the almost accidental chance that, having graduated from Yale in 1920, I was sent abroad to study archaeology at the American Academy in Rome. We even took field trips in those days and in a small way took part in diggings. Once you have swung a pickax that will reveal the curve of a street four thousand years covered over which was once an active, much-traveled highway, you are never quite the same again. You look at Times Square as a place about which you imagine some day scholars saying, "There appears to have been some kind of public center here."

ture. At the moments when they act out their personal joy and sadness, they present an abstract rendering of these emotions as they come to us all. They are allegorical figures, but, because what they represent is not a special quality or force but the complete sum of the human passions, and because also they speak in an ordinary manner without the aggrandizing self-consciousness of an Everyman, they are completely absorbing as characters in their own right. In attending, as it were, to the development of George and Emily, Wilder is concerned primarily with their virtues, but he does not omit the vices from the design of their personalities. Thus, for example, they delight in ice cream sodas, delay over their homework, and plan ahead for a profitable farm. These interests are nothing less than the deadly sins of gluttony, sloth, and avarice, yet so softened as to round out the design without rendering the boy and girl egregious. The point is that if we are to see ourselves in George and Emily, we must not be so dismayed that we avert our eyes. The two protagonists grow up in houses on adjacent properties, play together as children, fall in love with one another in adolescence, and marry as soon as they graduate from high school. Emily dies in childbirth after nine years of marriage, and as the play ends George grieves hopelessly beside her grave. That is all. But so basic to the life of every civilization are these experiences and the emotions they evoke that their theatrical impact is universally stunning.

THE UNIVERSALITY OF EVENTS

To extend the dimensions of the plot, Wilder employs images of vast numbers which with a lightly comic tone the Stage Manager pulls out of his capacious mind. In three years the sun comes up a thousand times, in long marriages husbands and wives may eat as many as fifty thousand meals together, every bride and groom have millions of ancestors, all of whom may be spectral guests at the wedding. To take the audience out of the present moment and move the play forward in time, Wilder permits the Stage Manager to use his omniscience in still another way: he mentions not only the past and present of the characters' lives, but their future, including, for many, the dates and circumstances of their deaths. At the end of the first act, after we have listened at length to his observations, we come to understand through the words of another figure, George Gibbs's young sister Re-

becca, that over all dates and places and activities such as
we have been hearing of, God eternally watches:

> REBECCA: I never told you about that letter Jane Crofut got
> from her minister when she was sick. The minister of her
> church in that town she was in before she came here. He
> wrote Jane a letter and on the envelope the address was like
> this: It said: Jane Crofut; The Crofut Farm; Grover's Corners;
> Sutton County; New Hampshire; United States of America.
>
> GEORGE: What's funny about that?
>
> REBECCA: But listen, it's not finished: the United States of
> America; Continent of North America; Western Hemisphere;
> the Earth; the Solar System; the Universe; the Mind of God—
> that's what it said on the envelope.
>
> GEORGE: What do you know!
>
> REBECCA: And the postman brought it just the same.
>
> GEORGE: What do you know!

Closely related to Gertrude Stein's comments on the gen-
eralizing tendency of Americans, this scene, in which the
life of Grover's Corners in all its pedestrian details has become the focus of cosmic forces, nevertheless projects a
quality which is pure Wilder. Each act contains a moment of
beauty and pathos, and of great familiarity, which moves the
play forward with a sureness of theatrical technique obviously beyond the ability of Miss Stein to inspire. In the first
act it is a scene between George and his father in which the
boy is scolded mildly for letting his mother chop wood for
the stove when he should be doing the job himself. In the
second act it is the acute bridal fear of Emily immediately
before the wedding ceremony as she expresses it in an an-
guished plea to George: "Well, if you love me, help me. All I
want is someone to love me." In the last, it is Emily's brief,
emotionally harrowing return to life and a reenactment of
her twelfth birthday. Unable to communicate with her family and suddenly aware that in the entire process of her life
the minutes have passed too quickly to be fully realized, she
cannot endure the massive grief now developing:

> EMILY: (*In a loud voice to the* STAGE MANAGER.) I can't. I can't
> go on. Oh! Oh! It goes too fast. We don't have time to look at
> one another. (*She breaks down sobbing. At a gesture from the*
> STAGE MANGER, MRS. WEBB *disappears.*) I didn't realize. So all
> that was going on and we never noticed. Take me back—up
> the hill—to my grave. But first: Wait! One more look. Good-
> by. Good-by, world. Good-by, Grover's Corners . . . Mama and

Papa. Good-by to clocks ticking . . . and Mama's sunflowers. And food and coffee. And new-ironed dresses and hot baths . . . and sleeping and waking up. Oh, earth, you're too wonderful for anybody to realize you. (*She looks toward the* STAGE MANAGER *and asks abruptly, through her tears:*) Do any human beings realize life while they live it?—every, every minute?

STAGE MANAGER: No. (*Pause.*) The saints and poets, maybe— they do some.

With this scene we come to a point to which Wilder always directs us: the belief that the cause of man's unhappiness is not his failure to achieve or sustain greatness, but his failure to delight in the beauty of ordinary existence. In the preface to his *Three Plays*, the collected edition of his major dramatic works, he writes forthrightly on this theme:

> *Our Town* is not offered as a picture of life in a New Hampshire Village; or as speculation about the conditions of life after death (that element I merely took from Dante's *Purgatory*). It is an attempt to find a value above all price for the smallest events in our daily life. . . . Moliére said that for the theatre all he needed was a platform and a passion or two. The climax of this play needs only five square feet of boarding and the passion to know what life means to us.

The people of Grover's Corners are the sort whose effect upon the world is slight, slighter even than the effect of such a man as George Brush [the protagonist in Wilder's novel *Heaven's My Destination*], since they never move away from their particular piece of the universe. For that reason they are the personages whose lives most clearly reflect the marvelousness of the unheroic.

Wilder's Affirmation of Life

Barnard Hewitt

Numerous drama critics have challenged Thornton Wilder's status as a great American playwright, criticizing his three major plays—*Our Town, The Skin of Our Teeth,* and *The Matchmaker*—as derivative, sentimental, and out of touch with the darker realities of American life. Barnard Hewitt argues in Wilder's defense that the playwright's purpose is not to dwell on the large and perplexing ugliness of life, but rather to show the joy of living, which includes the daily struggles of growing up. Hewitt suggests that the Stage Manager, who possesses the double vision of past and present, works to place these everyday, human joys and pains in the context of the eternal flow of life.

According to Hewitt, the lack of scenery in *Our Town* is not an affectation of the playwright but an integral part of Wilder's purpose to create a sense of the universal. Scenery and props would identify the action and tie it to a given time and place. Additionally, Hewitt reasons, the lack of scenery helps the audience to make rapid shifts from past to present and from life to death. Thornton Wilder's view of the theater is not to create illusion but to provide a structured pretense that allows the audience to collaborate in the dramatic creation.

Barnard Hewitt is a literary critic and author of *Theatre U.S.A. 1668 to 1957.*

The prefatory note to the volume, *Three Plays by Thornton Wilder,* states that he is regarded by many as America's greatest living playwright. We may discount this considerably as a publisher's exaggeration, but there is no question that his name will appear on almost anyone's list of major

Excerpted from Barnard Hewitt, "Thornton Wilder Says 'Yes,'" *Tulane Drama Review,* vol. 4, December 1959, pp. 110–20. Reprinted by permission of *The Drama Review,* Tisch School of the Arts, New York, N.Y.

contemporary American playwrights—and probably nearer the top than the bottom.

This is a little surprising when one stops to think that his reputation rests almost entirely on three plays, one of them an adaptation. True, he has written a number of one-act plays, one or two of which have become classics of the amateur theatre. He has translated André Obey's *Lucrèce* for Katharine Cornell and he has adapted *A Doll's House* for Ruth Gordon. His trilogy on the Alcestis story, *A Life in the Sun*, was seen at the Edinburgh Festival in 1957. But his name and fame as a playwright depend on *Our Town*, first produced in 1938, *The Skin of Our Teeth* in 1942, and *The Matchmaker* in 1954. A small output in twenty years.

Moreover, these three plays have not been universally hailed as masterpieces, or even as original contributions to American drama and theatre. On the contrary, both *The Skin of Our Teeth* and *Our Town* have been attacked as derivative. Joseph Campbell and Henry Morton Robinson, authors of the *Skeleton Key to Finnegan's Wake*, were shocked to discover that *The Skin of Our Teeth* drew a good deal from James Joyce's puzzling work and ended their inventory of the borrowings by suggesting that if the play shows genius it is the genius not of Wilder but of Joyce.

Julian Sawyer concurred about *The Skin of Our Teeth* and pointed out that *Our Town* owes a considerable debt to Gertrude Stein's *The Making of Americans*. He pronounced this stern judgment: "the superficial and escapist treatment that Thornton Wilder bestowed upon his all too derivative material makes him anything but a purloiner of the great thought, beauty, and feeling which constituted those works of art resulting from the genius of Gertrude Stein and James Joyce."

Francis Fergusson, writing in the *Sewanee Review* in 1956, although he expressed admiration for Wilder's theatrical virtuosity, pronounced him fundamentally sentimental and pretentious.

Wilder has been attacked too as a shallow optimist, out of touch with the dark realities of American life today. His plays have been extremely popular in Germany, as indeed elsewhere in Europe, since World War II, and when Wilder visited Germany . . . he received an enthusiastic welcome. Paul Fussell, Jr. in *The Nation*, noting this phenomenon with a cynical eye, observed that of living American writers Wilder is the least touched by the social, intellectual and psycholog-

ical currents of America as it is. Europeans, seeking a soothing picture of the country, upon which their own future appears so largely to depend, have seized not upon Williams or
Faulkner with their deep wells of envy, anger, hatred, and
terror but upon the mild Wilder. To quote Mr. Fussell: "Here,
gratifying the European image of what he should be, was the
American Writer, with all his folksy innocence of evil, with
all his touching devotion to Love, and with all his inspiring
and efficient optimism." According to Mr. Fussell, Thornton
Wilder is hoodwinking Europeans—who of course are asking to be hoodwinked. He offers them in *The Skin of Our
Teeth* a vitalistic, cosmic optimism out of tune with our time,
and in *Our Town* an image of America that is "pastoral, complacent, coy, charming, and entirely unreal.". . .

OUR TOWN AS A PLAY OF PEACE AND ACCEPTANCE

If *The Matchmaker* is a lively song in praise of adventure,
Our Town might be called a hymn to the humdrum. As
Wilder has said, "*Our Town* is not offered as a picture of life
in a New Hampshire village; or speculation about the conditions of life after death. . . . It is an attempt to find a value
above all price for the smallest events of daily life." *The
Matchmaker* is a play of extraordinary action, light-hearted
rebellion, and high spirits. *Our Town* is a play of everyday activity, poignant feeling, and the peace which comes with acceptance.

In spite of its success with audiences, or perhaps because
of that success, *Our Town* has been attacked by some critics
as sentimental, untrue. It presents a false picture, they say,
because it contains none of the ugliness of small-town life in
America as it exists and as it has been represented in the
drama by William Inge and in other literary media by Sherwood Anderson, Carl Sandburg, and Edwin Arlington
Robinson. [American literary critic] Eric Bentley has criticized the use of the Stage Manager as condescending to the
audience and as productive of repetition and platitude. The
disuse of scenery and properties has been termed quaint,
coy, and distracting.

The ugly side of American small-town life is not entirely
missing from *Our Town*. Simon Stimson, the drunken, disappointed organist is there. In a play by Tennessee Williams
or William Inge, he would be stage center. Wilder keeps
Simon close to the wings. His purpose is not to present a

complete picture of small-town life but rather through its little cycle of daily activity and its big cycle of birth, marriage, and death to discover for us the value of the ordinary in human life any time, anywhere, every time, everywhere. *Our Town*, though it contains little ugliness, does not evade the pain of life. It is full not only of the pleasure and joy of ordinary living but of the little troubles of growing up, the terror of youth before the mystery of marriage, and the anguish of the bereaved before the terminal fact of death. To have given more prominence to Simon Stimson and his like would only have distracted from Wilder's purpose.

THE STAGE MANAGER'S PERSPECTIVE

The frame supplied by the Stage Manager is essential to that purpose. The Stage Manager is not merely an easy means to exposition, to setting the scene in Grover's Corners. He is the principal means to the double vision, the intermeshing of past and present, which permeates the whole play, as Winfield Townley Scott has noted in "Our Town and the Golden Veil" in the *Virginia Quarterly Review*. Although the Stage Manager knows Grover's Corners well, he exists in our time. He can call in Professor Willard to place Grover's Corners and its inhabitants for us in the scale of geologic and historic time. He can himself remind us that Babylon once had two million people in it, and though all we know about them is the names of the kings and some copies of wheat contracts, every night all those families sat down to supper, and the father came home from work, and the smoke went up the chimney, same as in Grover's Corners, same as here. And he can glance into the future of Grover's Corners and tell us what is to change and what is to remain.

The double vision the Stage Manager permits is responsible for the play's two-fold effect. *Our Town* appears somehow to have to do simultaneously with very ordinary people and with the shining galaxies of stars, with the smallest of small towns and with the universe, with time and with eternity. Oddly enough, Grover's Corners and the Webbs and the Gibbs do not appear insignificant against the backdrop of eternity; they are not lost in the vastness of the universe. The daily routine and the individual life cycle of birth, marriage, and death are revealed as part of the eternal rhythm of the universe.

The Play's Purpose and the Absence of Scenery

The absence of scenery and of realistic properties in *Our Town* may strike the sophisticated playgoer as coy or the less sophisticated playgoer as quaint, and therefore prove distracting to both, but I believe not for long. If the play is reasonably well acted, one quickly accepts the convention and forgets that the real stove, the real dishes, the real newspaper are not there. And this convention is no affectation. It is integral to Wilder's concept. Although the action of the play takes place in a small town in New Hampshire at a specific time and it is concerned with individuals, yet it aims to illustrate a truth that holds for men and women everywhere, in the big city as well as the small town, and in every time, in 1938 or 1959 as well as in 1901. Scenery and realistic properties would have tied *Our Town* too firmly to the particular time and place, would have made it the nostalgic, sentimental play of life in the vanished American small town, for which it is sometimes mistaken. Thornton Wilder has said exactly this in another way:

> Emily's joys and griefs, her algebra lessons, her birthday presents—what are they when we consider all the billions of girls who have lived, who are living, and who will live? Each individual's assertion to an absolute reality can only be inner. . . . And here the method of staging finds its justification. . . . Our claim, our hope, our despair are in the mind—not in things, not in 'scenery.' The climax of this play needs only five square feet of boarding and the passion to know what life means to us.

It is hard to imagine how the climax of *Our Town* could be achieved at all under the conditions imposed by the presence of scenery. Without scenery, the transitions in scene can be as swift as the imagination, not only in time and place but back and forth from life to death. Emily has died in childbirth and she comes to take her place among the dead in the Grover's Corners cemetery. She learns that it is possible to return, to relive the past among the living, and she goes back, in spite of warnings from the dead and from the Stage Manager who says: "You not only live it but you watch yourself living it. And as you watch . . . you know what's going to happen afterwards." Emily has chosen to relive her twelfth birthday. From its beginning, every moment of that day is transfigured by her double awareness. Each moment is almost unbearably beautiful, and each moment goes so fast! Finally the dead Emily of fourteen years later cries: "Mama, just for a moment we're happy. Let's look at one another!" But the living have no time to look and they cannot hear the voice out of the future. Emily, unable to bear the happiness and the pain, flees back to the disinterested dead. And she cries out to the Stage Manager, "Do human beings ever realize life while they live it? every, every minute?" "No," he answers, "The saints and poets maybe—they do some."

Thus, *Our Town* asserts the value of human life, no matter how apparently trivial, no matter how apparently insignificant. It does so, not by ignoring or belittling change and death, but by reminding us that change is necessary to the recognition of beauty and that death in a very fundamental way gives meaning to life. *Optimism*, even unmodified by the derogatory adjective *shallow*, does not seem to me quite the word to describe this view of the world. I should call it *affirmation.* . . .

WILDER'S THEATER OF MAKE-BELIEVE

If Thornton Wilder is an optimist, his is no shallow optimism. He recognizes that pain, cruelty, failure, and death are a part of living but he feels strongly that they can never completely define life. Gerald Weales has observed that Wilder, like the heroine of his novel *The Woman of Andros*, seems to say, "I have known the worst that the world can do . . . nevertheless, I praise the world and all living." He says "yes" to life.

Thornton Wilder says "yes" to the theatre also. He recognizes and accepts the fact that theatre is a collaborative art, that director and actors necessarily intervene their bodies, minds, and imaginations between the playwright and his vision of his play. In his essay "Some Thoughts on Playwriting," he says he seeks "to organize the play in such a way that its strength lies not in appearances beyond his control, but in the succession of events and in the unfolding of an idea, in narration." The details of the physical realization of his play he is happy to leave to actors and director. He recognizes too that a play is addressed not to individuals but to a group, and he accepts the fact that the "group-mind imposes upon him the necessity of treating materials understandable by the larger number."

Above all, Thornton Wilder believes in the theatricality of the theatre. The theatre, he says, is a world not of illusion but of pretense, of make-believe. It lives by conventions, that is, by agreed upon falsehoods, by permitted lies. "When it tries to assert that the personages in the action 'really are,' really inhabit such and such rooms, really suffer from such and such emotions, it loses rather than gains credibility." Convention, he maintains, provokes the spectator to collaborate in the dramatic creation, and it raises the action from the specific to the general. The element of pretense reinforces the continual effort of the stage to present generalized truth.

Of course, the theatre of "illusion," as Wilder uses the term, is also a theatre of pretense. No one mistakes its personages for real people. And like the theatre of "make-believe," it depends upon conventions—agreed upon falsehoods, permitted lies. But its conventions are different conventions. They tend to make the audience a spectator rather than a collaborator; they tend to make the drama particular rather than general.

The theatre of "illusion"—as opposed to the theatre of "make-believe"—is, in a way, theatre that denies itself. Not only the realistic theatre of producers and directors Belasco and Stanislavsky but the symbolistic theatre of Gordon Craig and Adolphe Appia seeks to create by means of text, actors, scenery, and light a world separate from the audience—not the world of the theatre, but the world of Peter Grimm or Madame Ranevsky or Hamlet or Tristan and Isolde. The proscenium arch is not only the symbol of that separation but the principal means whereby the illusion is created.

Thornton Wilder's plays in one way or another break down the barrier of the proscenium arch. They involve the spectator directly by frankly making him once more a participant in a theatrical experience. These plays have been and continue to be highly successful. They point the way the living theatre should go, for if it is to survive as anything but a luxury for the few, it must discard the conventions of "illusion" and revive the older conventions of "make-believe." It should leave the creation of "illusion" to the moving picture and to television, both of which are infinitely better equipped for it. The theatre should reaffirm itself as an art of "pretense" not of "illusion," of living actors not real people, and of an active not a passive audience.

Thornton Wilder is important in today's American theatre because he is a believer, a yea-sayer. He says "yes" to the life of the theatre, still struggling to escape the strangling embrace of realism and illusion. And through the theatre he says "yes" to human life. In what sometimes seems an unbroken chorus of aggression and rejection by contemporary American playwrights, his is one strong, affirmative voice.

Everyday Existence in *Our Town*

Bernard F. Dukore

Bernard F. Dukore writes that the characters in *Our Town* and the town itself, Grover's Corners, New Hampshire, are archetypes of the American experience, an experience that is homespun, egalitarian, and democratic. Despite the fact that life in Grover's Corners is archetypal, the playwright does not hide the negative or bleak side of small-town life: There is a jail, the choirmaster is stultified by the lack of artistic creativity, lives are wasted by World War I.

Dukore maintains that Wilder's central theme revolves around the need to celebrate the simplest events of life and to acknowledge that the commonplace has value. Wilder emphasizes the fact that life rushes by and people have a tendency to take it for granted, unaware that everyday existence is precious and should be savored. Wilder accentuates the significance of ordinary experiences by placing them against a larger cosmic backdrop. Dukore suggests the best example of this is the address of the letter to Jane Crofut at her farm, which goes on to include the United States of America and ultimately the universe and the mind of God.

Bernard Dukore is a professor of drama and theater at the University of Hawaii. He has written extensively about the theater, playwrights, dramatic theory, and criticism.

Appropriately, because a major theme of *Our Town* is the transcendent value of the apparently banal, our analysis starts with two commonplace factors. First, the Stage Manager immediately names the play's author, director and chief actors: thereby indicating to the audience that the play

Excerpted from Bernard F. Dukore, *American Dramatists, 1918–1945* (New York: Grove Press, 1984). Reprinted by permission of Macmillan Press Ltd.

is a fiction, not reality, and also thwarting our predisposition to regard the production in realistic terms. Second, he very early suggests that Grover's Corners, New Hampshire, to which the title refers, is not only the characters' town but ours as well. As a review reveals, the first production dramatised what the text hints: 'The house lights are still on when he first saunters across the stage and begins to put chairs in place. Now and then he looks out to see how the audience is coming, and takes a glance at his watch.' As he casually talks about Grover's Corners, 'The audience, taken directly into the narrator's confidence, becomes part of the town's population' (*New York Sun*). In Act III, set on a nearby hilltop, the Stage Manager, *'pointing down in the audience'*, states, 'there, quite a ways down, is Grover's Corners'. At the play's end, the link is complete. 'Most everybody's asleep in Grover's Corners.' Then: 'Eleven o'clock in Grover's Corners. —You get a good rest, too. Good night.' On Broadway in 1938, when plays began at 8.30 P.M., *Our Town* rang down at about eleven. Grover's Corners time has become the audience's time, the play truly *our* town.

GROVER'S CORNERS AND THE AMERICAN EXPERIENCE

Grover's Corners is not real but prototypical: a fiction and part of 'our' American experience. Democratically and with artful simplicity, Wilder addresses *Our Town* to an undifferentiated audience of a classless society. The play's values are those of the ideal American small town in the stable, pre-internationalised period before the First World War: democratic, egalitarian, middle-class, neighbourly and homespun. Wilder stresses Grover's Corner's community, not its potential divisiveness. While it has rich and poor, 'we try to take care of those that can't help themselves and those that can we leave alone'. In the first scene Doc Gibbs returns from the poorer section of town, where before dawn he helped deliver twins; he chats in democratic, neighbourly fashion with the newsboy and the man who delivers milk. Most of the townsfolk, minister included, tolerate the choirmaster's drunkenness. Repeatedly, characters call the town nice, unremarkable, ordinary and unimportant. If Grover's Corners were less ordinary it would be less archetypal. Its values are traditional, and as the state's name implies they are both American ('New') and also extend beyond the Union ('Hampshire'). The community is stable. 'Mortality and birth-rates are constant' and as late as 1913 it has no burglaries. Like life, Grover's Corners changes, though in small ways: 10 per cent of its high school graduates settle elsewhere; *almost* everyone marries; automobiles *begin* to replace horses. Essentially, however, 'things don't change much'.

The characters' experiences are typical. The older children of neighbouring families, George Gibbs and Emily Webb, attend school, marry and raise a family; she dies. Partly through the Gibbses and Webbs, but also independently of them—for the Stage Manager, literally managing the events on stage, introduces other characters to deliver different views of the town and sometimes plays their roles; begins and ends scenes to demonstrate characters or themes ('That'll do' concludes one); omnisciently explains ideas to the audience, albeit in a dry, folksy manner—Wilder focuses not on individuals but on 'our' archetypal town. Never sectarian or particularly theological (or for that matter grammatical), the play's religious views are homocentric and humanistic: 'everybody knows in their bones that *something* is eternal, and that something has to do with human beings'.

Our Town is ideal in the sense of archetype, not because it ignores unpleasantness. Emphasising kindliness and goodness, it does not hide the bleaker side of American small town life. Grover's Corners has a jail; while its citizens appreciate the beauties of nature, they are virtually uncultured (among the few books they read is Defoe's *Robinson Crusoe*, which celebrates the middle station of life); no fit place for an artist, the small town's stultification drives the choirmaster to drink and suicide. Mrs Webb's concern for her daughter points to its neglect of proper sex education: 'there's something downright cruel about sending our girls out into marriage this way. I hope some of her girl friends have told her a thing or two. It's cruel, I know, but I couldn't bring myself to say anything. I went into it blind as a bat myself. The whole world's wrong, that's what's the matter.' Nor does *Our Town* neglect darker aspects of life that go beyond a small town, including the waste of lives by war. Telling the audience what the future holds for characters other than the Gibbses and Webbs, the Stage Manager says of the newsboy Joe Crowell, Jr, 'Joe was a very bright fellow. He graduated with honours and got a scholarship to Boston Tech.—M.I.T., that is [Massachusetts Institute of Technology]. But the War broke out and Joe died in France. All that education for nothing.' Wilder, who a year earlier had rendered Henrik Ibsen's *A Doll's House* into English for actress Ruth Gordon, questions the institution of marriage. 'I've married two hundred couples in my day', the Stage Manager in the role of clergyman tells the audience. 'Do I believe in it? I don't know.'. . .

THE CELEBRATION OF DAILY LIFE

As Wilder says, *Our Town* aims 'to find a value above all price for the smallest events in our daily life' (Preface to *Three Plays*). Against the millennia of earthly existence, quotidian events might seem to lack significance; yet because life is fleeting each moment is precious and the apparently trivial details of an individual's life acquire value through one's awareness of them. *Our Town* celebrates the simplest, least pretentious type of life. If the most commonplace aspects of life have priceless value, consider the worth of what is not ordinary. When the Stage Manager says, before we see Doc Gibbs in 1901, that he will die in 1930 and have a hospital named for him, his mundane actions and chats become heightened in the spectator's eyes. At times, such as the introduction of the soda fountain scene, the Stage Manager establishes this perspective: 'I want you to try and remember what it was like when you were fifteen or sixteen. For some reason it is very hard to do: those days when even the little things in life could be almost too exciting to bear.' Wilder also demonstrates unawareness. Because infants become children who become adolescents who become adults, one might expect parents—who often remark on the rapidity of these changes—to be aware of the value of small moments of life. Not so. Such exchanges as this, between daughter and mother, are all too frequent: 'I'm the brightest girl in school for my age. I have a wonderful memory.' 'Eat your breakfast.'

The fullest expression of this theme occurs in Act III, when the dead Emily receives an opportunity to visit the living, but with a painful condition: she is both participant and observer, living the moment and watching herself live it. She selects a relatively unimportant day. To Wilder, the most insignificant events of life are awesome. Returning to life on her twelfth birthday, she sees with wonder what will soon disappear: a pre-renovated drug store, a pre-automotive livery stable, a white fence 'that used to' surround her house, and her mother's youth ('I didn't know Mama was ever that young'). As onlooker, she sees, in the crucial sense of perceiving, that people do not pause to be happy or to express their love for each other. Life goes by too quickly. Soon, she can no longer bear to remain among the living and bids farewell to what, too late, she has come to appreciate: 'Good-by, world. Good-by, Grover's Corners . . . Mama and Popa. Good-by to clocks ticking . . . and Mama's sunflowers. And food and coffee. And new-ironed dresses and hot baths . . . and sleeping and waking up. Oh, earth, you're too wonderful for anybody to realize you.' As Wilder explains in his 1930 novel *The Woman of Andros*, in which a character returns to life under the same conditions as Emily: 'the living too are dead and [. . .] we can only be said to be alive in those moments when our hearts are conscious of our treasure'. Emily asks the Stage Manager, 'Do any human beings ever realize life while they live it?—every, every minute?' His answer: 'No. (*Pause*) The saints and poets, maybe—they do some.' Despite its poignance the scene is not a tearjerker. In his Preface to the Acting Edition Wilder advises the actress that the dominant emotion is one 'of wonder rather than of sadness'. Another factor that helps to prevent excessive sentimentality is non-didacticism. He does not admonish the audience to become like saints and poets. Furthermore, since the Stage Manager's 'No' applies to most people, what might inspire us might also depress us.

OUR TOWN AS A MICROCOSM

Our Town is a microcosm. Wilder ('A Preface to *Our Town*') presents 'the life of a village against the life of the stars'. With microscope and telescope, as it were, he dramatises ordinary life against a cosmic background. The play's three acts take place on four specific days, including the flashback, from 1899 (the year after a long economic depression) to 1913 (the year before the First World War). The Stage Manager offers a wealth of detail, including date, time of day, location of buildings and names on tombstones. He relates these to the universe: latitude and longitude, prehistoric fossils, 'sun and moon and stars'. As Wilder points out (Preface to *Three Plays*), 'The recurrent words in this play [. . .] are "hundreds", "thousands", and "millions"'. Husbands and wives eat thousands of meals together, for instance, millions of ancestors gather at a wedding. He juggles time. We observe the events of 7 May 1901, for example, but the Stage Manager addresses the audience in time that is its 'now' while a copy of the play is being placed in a cornerstone of a building for people a thousand years later and he refers to the automobile that will arrive five years from the play's 'now', life in Babylon thousands of years earlier, and rocks that are millions of years old.

The play's most celebrated juxtaposition of specific and universal is a letter addressed to 'Jane Crofut; The Crofut Farm; Grover's Corners; Sutton County; New Hampshire; United States of America. [. . .] Continent of North America; Western Hemisphere; the Earth; the Solar System; the Universe; the Mind of God.' Emblematic of the play's light tone is a teenage girl's comment on the address: 'And the postman brought it just the same'. Wilder goes further: he places *Our Town* in the larger context of western literary tradition. This letter, the finale of Act I, expands a passage in [Irish novelist] James Joyce's *Portrait of the Artist as a Young Man*. A reference in Act II combines the names of Mark Twain's most famous characters: 'Everybody always says that Tom Huckins drives [the hardware store wagon] like a crazy man'. Act III repeats a portion, mentioned earlier, of Wilder's novel *The Woman of Andros*, which has Graeco-Roman sources.

The structure embodies a universal pattern: Act I, which early on reports birth, is titled 'The Daily Life'; the subjects of Act II are 'Love and Marriage'; Act III is about death, which illuminates life. Ritualistically, each act contains milkman, paperboy and breakfast. Binding the acts ritualistically is an appropriate song, 'Blessed be the tie that binds', rendered during choir practice in Act I, at the wedding in Act II, and during the funeral in Act III.

Wilder's Search for Essentials

John Mason Brown

John Mason Brown suggests that the lack of scenery in *Our Town* requires audience members to use their imagination and, in the process, get involved in the creation of the play. By stripping the stage to its barest essentials, Wilder is emphasizing his intent to depict the fundamental elements of living. According to Brown, the playwright reveals the basic pattern behind all human existence and lays bare the essential emotions underlying the shared experience of living.

Brown argues that Wilder was uninterested in presenting social dilemmas and problems of modern society, nor was he concerned with current issues of economics, personalities, or events. He was searching for that which is common to all hearts. Brown concludes that the true setting of *Our Town* is the human heart.

John Mason Brown was a literary critic for *Saturday Review* and the editor and drama critic for *Theatre Arts Monthly*. He is the author of many works including *The Modern Theater in Revolt* and *American Theater as Seen by Its Critics*.

No scenery is required for this play. Perhaps a few dusty flats may be seen leaning against the brick wall at the back of the stage. . . . The Stage Manager not only moves forward and withdraws the few properties that are required, but he reads from a typescript the lines of all the minor characters. He reads them clearly, but with little attempt at characterization, scarcely troubling himself to alter his voice, even when he responds in the person of a child or a woman. As the curtain rises the Stage Manager is leaning lazily against the proscenium pillar at the audience's left. He is smoking.

The chances are that if, during the course of one of those parlor games which offer to hostesses and guests alike an ideal retreat from bridge and conversation, some playgoers were asked to identify the play for which these stage directions were intended, they would not guess *Julius Caesar* at the Mercury. Yet they might be sufficiently foolhardy, in this season of sceneryless scripts, to pick upon Mr. Blitzstein's *The Cradle Will Rock* or Mr. Wilder's *Our Town.* If they choose *Our Town*, because the demand for a Stage Manager, leaning against the proscenium and smoking a pipe, brought the genial Frank Craven to their minds, they would at least be "getting warm," as the gamesters have it. Still they would be very far from being "hot." Although Mr. Wilder is the author of these stage directions, *Our Town* is not the play for which they were intended. They were written for a charming one-act of his called *The Happy Journey to Trenton and Camden* which was copyrighted in 1931 and which can be found not only in a volume of his short plays called *The Long Christmas Dinner* but also in [American journalist and writer] Professor Alexander Woollcott's first *Reader.*

I go back to Mr. Wilder's earlier usage of this frankly presentational form only because some theatregoers have been tempted to talk and write about *Our Town* as if it were a production which found Mr. Wilder and Mr. Harris trying to climb upon the Mercury's band wagon. It is important to note that when Mr. Wilder sent the script of *The Happy Journey* to Washington seven years ago, all he was attempting to copyright was the use to which he put this particular form in this particular script, and not the form itself. What really matters in all art is this very thing. Forms and subjects are comparatively few. Yet they can be made as various as are the talents of the many artists who have repossessed them. . . .

The form Mr. Wilder has used is as old as the theatre's ageless game of "let's pretend" and as new as the last time it has been employed effectively. The cooperation it asks an audience to contribute is at heart the very same cooperation which the most realistic and heavily documented productions invite playgoers to grant. The major difference is one of degree. Both types of production depend in the last analysis upon their audiences to supply that final belief which is the mandate under which all theatrical illusion operates. The form Mr. Wilder uses is franker, that is all. It does not at-

> **WILDER'S LOVE OF THE STAGE**
>
> *In a September 17, 1965, article entitled "A Hermit in Chilmark" for* Vineyard Gazette, *Peter S. McGhee records Thornton Wilder's love of theater.*
>
> "I'm really stage struck. The stage is the greatest of all art forms—one in which society sits shoulder to shoulder and sees an imaginary story about the human condition. In paintings, you can be alone and get everything out of a picture; at a concert people listen alone, there is not nearly the pooling of judgement that there is in the theater—an audience of one at a play would be impossible."

tempt to hide the fact that it is make-believe. Instead it asks its audiences to do some of the work, to enter openly and gladly into the imaginative conspiracy known as the successful staging of a play.

OUR TOWN AS THEATRICAL ILLUSION

What such a drama as Mr. Wilder's does, of course, is to strip theatrical illusion down to its essentials. Mr. Wilder has the best of good reasons for so doing. What he has done in *Our Town* is to strip life down to its essentials, too. There is nothing of the "stunt" about the old-new form he has employed. His form is the inevitable one his content demands. Indeed, so inevitable is it, and hence so right, that I, for one, must confess I lost all awareness of it merely as a form a few minutes after Mr. Craven had begun to set the stage by putting a few chairs in place. There have been those who have been bothered because the pantomime was not consistent, because real umbrellas were carried and no visible lawn-mower was pushed, because naturalistic offstage sounds serve as echoes to the actions indicated on stage. I was not one of the bothered. I found myself surrendering, especially during the first two acts, to the spell of the beautiful and infinitely tender play Mr. Wilder has written.

John Anderson has likened *Our Town* to India's rope trick. He has pointed out it is the kind of play at which you either see the boy and the rope, or you don't. Although I refuse to admit there is anything of the fakir's touch in *Our Town*, I think I understand what Mr. Anderson means. Mr. Wilder's is, from the audience point of view, an exceptionally personal play. More than most plays, since by its sweet simplicity it seeks to get in contact with the inmost nerves of our living, it is the kind of drama which depends upon what we bring to it.

Mr. Wilder's play is concerned with the universal importance of those unimportant details which figure in the lives of men and women everywhere. His Grover's Corners is a New Hampshire town inhabited by decent New England people. The very averageness of these quiet, patient people in the point at which our lives and all living become a part of their experience. Yet Mr. Wilder's play involves more than a New England township. It burrows into the essence of the growing-up, the marrying, the living, and the dying of all of us who sit before it and are included by it. The task to which Mr. Wilder has set himself is one which [English novelist Thomas] Hardy had in mind in a far less human, more grandiose way, when he had the Chorus in *The Dynasts* say:

> We'll close up Time, as a bird its van,
> We'll traverse Space, as Spirits can,
> Link pulses severed by leagues and years,
> Bring cradles into touch with biers.

Mr. Wilder succeeds admirably in doing this. He shows us the simple pattern behind all simple living. He permits us to share in the inevitable anguishes and joys, the hopes and cruel separations to which men have been heir since the smoke puffed up the chimneys in Greece.

THE ESSENTIAL EXPERIENCE OF LIVING

To my surprise I have encountered the complaint that Mr. Wilder's Grover's Corners is not like Middletown, U.S.A. It lacks brothels, race riots, huge factories, front-page scandals, social workers, union problems, lynchings, agitators, and strikes. The ears of its citizens are more familiar with the song of the robin than they are with the sirens of hurrying police cars. Its young people are stimulated to courtship by moonlight rather than by moonshine. They drink soda water instead of gin. Their rendezvous are held in drug stores rather than in night clubs. Their parents are hard-working people. They are quiet, self-respecting, God-fearing Yankees who get up early to do their day's work and meet their responsibilities and their losses without whining. The church organist may tipple, and thereby cause some gossip. But he is a neighbor, and the only good-neighbor policy they care about begins at home.

They do not murder or steal, borrow or beg, blackmail or oppress. Furthermore, they face the rushing years without complaints as comparatively happy mortals. Therefore to certain realists they seem unreal. "No historian," one critic has written "has ever claimed that a town like Mr. Wilder's was ever so idyllic as to be free from intolerance and injustice." Mr. Wilder does not make this claim himself. His small-town editor admits Grover's Corners is "little better behaved than most towns." Neither is Mr. Wilder working as the ordinary historian works. His interests are totally different interests.

He is not concerned with social trends, with economic conditions, with pivotal events, or glittering personalities. He sings not of arms and the man, but of those small events which loom so large in the daily lives of each of us, and which are usually unsung. His interest is the unexceptional, the average, the personal. His preoccupation is what lies beneath the surface and the routine of our lives, and is common to all our hearts and all our experience. It is not so much of the streets of a New England Town he writes as of the clean white spire which rises above them.

WILDER'S VISION

There are hundreds of fat books written each year on complicated subjects by authors who are not writers at all. But the ageless achievement of the true writers has always been to bring a new illumination to the simplest facts of life. That illumination has ever been a precious talent given only to a few. It is because Mr. Wilder brings this illumination to his picture of Grover's Corners that I admire *Our Town.* New Hampshire is the state which can claim Mr. Wilder's village, but his vision of it has been large enough to include all of us, no matter where we may come from, among its inhabitants. Personally, I should as soon think of condemning the Twenty-third Psalm because it lacks the factual observation of [American novelist] Sinclair Lewis and the social point of view of [American author and critic] Granville Hicks as I would of accusing *Our Town* of being too unrealistically observed.

Anyone who hears only the milk bottles clink when early morning has come once again to Grover's Corners has not heard what Mr. Wilder wants them to hear. These milk bottles are merely the spokesmen of time, symbols for the bigness of little things. In terms of the Gibbses and the Webbs,

Mr. Wilder gives the pattern of repetition of each small day's planning, each small life's fruition and decline. He makes us feel the swift passage of the years, our blindness in meeting their race, the sense that our lives go rushing past so quickly that we have scarcely time in which to hold our breaths.

Only once does he fail us seriously. This is in his scene in the bleak graveyard on the hill. Although he seeks there to create the image of the dead who have lost their interest in life, he has not been able to capture the true greatness of vision which finds them at last unfettered from the minutiae of existence. Both his phrasing and his thinking are inadequate here. He chills the living by removing his dead even from compassion.

Nonetheless Mr. Wilder's is a remarkable play, one of the sagest, warmest, and most deeply human scripts to have come out of our theatre. It is the kind of play which suspends us in time, making us weep for our own vanished youth at the same time we are sobbing for the short-lived pleasures and sufferings which we know await our children. Geographically *Our Town* can be found at an imaginary place known as "Grover's Corners, Sultan County, New Hampshire, United States of America, Continent of North America, Western Hemisphere, the Earth, the Solar System, the Universe, the Mind of God." Mr. Wilder's play is laid in no imaginary place. It becomes a reality in the human heart.

Time in *Our Town*

Helmut Papajewski

Helmut Papajewski explains how Wilder immerses his
audience in the everyday movement of time. In the
first two acts of *Our Town*, for example, events portray
time as an ever-flowing passage of small units. Only
the Stage Manager has a larger view of time in which
he can comment on the past, present, and future. According to Papajewski, Wilder suggests that death interrupts the ordinary passage of time and exposes the
metaphysical nature of the finality of time.

The characters' common lives play out in an unvary-
ing pattern of normality, philosophically dependent on
everyday truisms like "It is unnatural to be alone." Papajewski argues that despite the smallness of their world,
the characters place a value on their identity because it
connects them to the past and helps them define reality.
The characters are not, however, individualized; all are
mediocre and represent types. George and Emily, for
example, are generalized and used by Wilder to portray
the traits of youth. When Emily returns after death, she
realizes that the human inclination to cling to repeti-
tious and familiar events blinds people from a shared
knowledge of how precious life is.

Helmut Papajewski is the author of a German
study on Wilder's works.

The individual acts of [*Our Town*] and the simple human activities in them give us the schedule of life in this town. At
5:45 A.M. is the departing whistle of the early train to Boston;
soon after that the deliveries of milk and newspapers; then
the mothers get up to make the children's breakfast; and the
children go to school.

All this is presented to us in an exceedingly familiar way
by means of whistles, ringing of bells, and calling. Yet the
end effect has a certain subtlety: the audience has the im-

pression of the constant passage of a segment of time. But this span of time moves in small time units. The view of time expressed in this First Act of *Our Town* is elucidated by a passage in one of Wilder's early works. In *Pullman Car Hiawatha* the stage manager says that the minutes are gossips, the hours philosophers, and the years theologians. This is paralleled in a later phase of Wilder's works, in *The Skin of Our Teeth*, where each of the late hours is interpreted by means of a passage from Spinoza, Plato, or Aristotle.

THE PASSAGE OF TIME

The First Act presents the time of bustling activity. The stage manager looks on all this with his watch in his hand. But the instrument that is man's best aid in reckoning time gives him no idea of the reality of time itself.

In the First Act the passage of time plays the great role. In Act Two there is, at the beginning, a reference to this in the fact that the attrition of time is made good by new births. Nature is the great adversary of time: "Nature's been pushing and contriving in other ways, too: a number of young people fell in love and got married." There was a certain hint of this kind also in Act One that Wilder may even have meant mischievously, when we are told on Dr. Gibbs' first appearance that he is returning from the delivery of twins. This notation, incidentally, shows the stage manager is having a positively confusing knowledge of time in all its phases. Dr. Gibbs is introduced in one act that takes place in the year 1901. At the same time, however, the stage manager reports in the past tense that Dr. Gibbs died in 1930 and that later a hospital in town was named after him. The stage manager, the sapient one, has the present, past and future time equally at his disposal.

The Second Act has, however, another function. In Act One the Gibbs and Webb families live self-contained lives side by side with each other. Now they are linked together by the wedding of their children. A lasting bond has been created, which will, however, as we soon learn, be broken by the death of one of the parties. Time is not only a stream constantly flowing in small units; it also creates things that are final.

The key image in the plot of Act Two was the long middle aisle leading to the altar. In place of the parallel action of two families there is common action. In the Third Act there is again separation. The rows of chairs indicating graves dominate one side of the stage.

Wilder further emphasizes this theme of community and separation—sometimes ironically—by having the hymn "Blessed Be the Tie That Binds" played or sung four times. First it is sung in Act One by housewives at a church rehearsal. Then it is whistled by Emily's father when she tells him of the letter with the strange address. At the wedding of George and Emily (both of whom are very nervous before the ceremony) it is the choral hymn. Lastly, it is the hymn chosen for Emily's burial.

EVERYDAY LIFE AT GROVER'S CORNERS

Finally, Wilder uses the play to illustrate his view of identity and time. It is precisely the interweaving of the everyday and the metaphysical world that serves to illuminate this question.

The entire play begins—as we saw—with a day that is not exceptional, indeed, a day of exemplary mediocrity; and the life of the characters has in its entire course nothing out of the ordinary, despite a few accents that are "of the hour." We know soon after the play has begun how everything is going to end, not because the play treats a familiar literary fable, but because it is a treatment of our ordinary life. There are hardly any differences in this usual sameness in the course of world history: in remote antiquity it is the same as in New England, we are told. In its concrete details, and in its political behavior, daily life in the various periods of world history may have been different, but in its essential everyday manifestations it remains the same.

There were also so-called exciting factors for the generation living in the United States in the nineteen-thirties. The stage manager makes reference to the Versailles Treaty and to Lindbergh's flight across the ocean. But they are less important for evaluating the man of the time than is his everyday life, which determines him as an anthropological type. A play like *Our Town* which says something about this should be placed in the cornerstone of the new building when a new Bank of Grover's Corners is built, so that "people in those years from now will know a few simple facts about us."

Among these "simple facts" are the banal statements that are here set forth, and the conversations which are so simple in their words and content but are also, through an unerring instinct, so effective on the stage. An example of this is the almost identical conversations on the weather of May 9, 1901, July 7, 1901, and February 11, 1899. Truisms such as "It is unnatural to be alone" are repeated over and over in a number of variations, for in the final analysis the truisms rule the day.

The usual trend of American drama in Wilder's time seems in this play to have completely altered its direction. The abnormal, which so often dominated the stage, is here replaced by an almost unrelieved normality.

IDENTITY ISSUES IN THE PLAY

The play is largely without effect if the audience is not willing to identify itself with the play's content. To one who does make this identification, the "little world" of American academic life is his world, in which the so-called "events" have only an illustrative force. It is strange enough that the members of such a world should still place a value on identity. But the consciousness of identity is at the same time the force that keeps them attached to the old, and makes them so often timid toward every change. Reality is for them a life-devouring power of custom.

Personal identity in this play is not very strongly individualized; the author's characters largely run to type. At the very start, through the agency of the stage manager, Wilder reduces any excessive expectations. From these first statements, the audience cannot expect to find any extraordinary people in this play: "Nice town, y'know what I mean? Nobody very remarkable ever come out of it—s'far as we know." The complete mediocrity of this town is clear from the somewhat euphemistic term "nice town," followed by the stage manager's rhetorical question as to an understanding between himself and the audience.

There are of course individual traits in George and Emily, but—as with Rebecca and Wally—they are made to typify youth; this is brought home to us all the more by the parallel scenes, in which almost the same words are used. The adults, too, have one common denominator: Mrs. Webb and Mrs. Gibbs in their almost complete absorption in their household cares, and Dr. Gibbs and Mr. Webb, who in their historical hobbies (the Napoleonic period, early American history) hardly differ from each other in any essential respect.

But despite their extensive absorption in the type, the persons in the play continue to hold fast to their identity, which they lose only with death. Thereafter, to the outward eye, they continue to appear as bearers of one or another of the many Anglo-Saxon names—Gibbs, Webb, Hersey, etc.—un-

LIBERATED TIME IN *OUR TOWN*

In a 1939 interview in the August 13 New York Times, *Thornton Wilder explains to John Franchey his redefined and expanded sense of time in* Our Town.

My experience with *Our Town* convinces me that the notion of time as immutable and consecutive action is not the only one. In *Our Town* time was scrambled, liberated.

"What I cannot at all share is the belief that events begin to have a significance only at that moment when the curtain goes up or a writer launches his opening paragraph; or that the significance has come to a full stop at the instant the curtain drops or finis is written.

"Does it seem vague? Well, let me illustrate what I am trying to do in my plays. I am searching for a new form in which there will be a perpetual counterpoint between the detailed episode of daily life—the meal, the chat, the courtship and the funeral—and the ever-present references to geological time and a distant future for the millions of people who have re-peated these moments. . . .

"I know you're wondering why. . . . And I'll tell you. The twentieth-century mind recognizes that mankind is not the cen-ter of the universe and at the same time is frightened by the sense of the countless repetitions of all human vicissitudes. This, I think, has caused a new sense of emphasis in narration. . . .

"Don't get me wrong, . . . I still have a profound respect for time and chronology. I get hungry at noon with amazing regu-larity."

til finally relegated to the alphabetical order of a cemetery. Inwardly, however, they have difficulty getting released from their identity.

EMILY'S VIEW OF LIFE

In the Third Act this is made clear in the fate of Emily. Here for the first time in one of his dramas Wilder treats the ques-tion of the return of the dead to earth. Emily is present at her own burial and speaks with the deceased. She is still uneasy and nervous, in contrast to the other dead, who have a large measure of poise and detachment: "The dead sit in a quiet without stiffness, and in a patience without listlessness," so the stage directions tell us at the outset. Mother Gibbs must admonish Emily: "Just wait and be patient." Even though the dead have not yet by any means lost their identity, they have nonetheless gained great peace. But they still have interest in some things, whether by way of liking or dislike. One of them likes to hear church hymns, and Mrs. Soames, who sees a stunt in all familiar events, still shows some cheerful receptiveness when familiar occasions present themselves, the burial not excluded.

Emily now already begins to realize something: "I never realized before how troubled and how . . . how in the dark live persons are." Living people's inability to see has already become clear to her, but—despite the dead Mrs. Gibbs' warnings—Emily has not yet gained patience and detachment enough to be able to renounce life entirely. She expects a festive day of life to give human warmth and great earthly radiance. Deep familiarity with the happy everyday things and the expectation of great sympathetic and consuming human love make a return to her former life seem urgently desirable to her. She is forced to recognize that absorption in everyday cares do not allow man to share in true living.

Emily's conclusion from a renewed earthly experience is: "That's all human beings are!—Just blind people. . . . That's what it was to be alive. To move about in a cloud of ignorance; to go up and down trampling on the feelings of those . . . of those about you. To spend and waste time as though you had a million years. To be always at the mercy of one self-centered passion, or another," adds Simon Stimson.

Her earlier question to the stage manager was: "Do any human beings ever realize life while they live it?—every, every minute?" The answer of the stage manager is almost completely negative: "No.—The saints and poets, maybe— they do some." What the poets had to say is—leaving aside everything that is purely poetic and consequently of value by reason of its beauty of expression, and considering what they say purely as a metaphysical utterance—not very much. But they are in a position to grasp the brevity and the wonder of life, and possibly to portray the intensity of relations between humans, as well as the joy in the reflected splendor of earthly life.

CHAPTER 3

Style and Criticism

READINGS ON
OUR TOWN

The Concept of Truth in *Our Town*

Thornton Wilder

In a preface to a collection of his plays, Thornton
Wilder argues that drama has the ability to awaken in
the audience what it means to be alive. He laments,
however, that drama in his own age has sacrificed the
ability to generate these powerful feelings, instead presenting plays that are soothing and passively diver-
sionary. According to Wilder, this weakening of the
theater stems from the nineteenth-century rise of a
middle-class society. The newly affluent did not want
hard or direct answers to life; instead, they demanded
theatrical presentations that justified their status and
reaffirmed their conformity to rules of decorum.
Hence, they settled for the softness of melodrama and
sentimental theater.

For Wilder, a successful drama must exercise its
inherent capacity to represent collective truths that
emerge from common experience. In *Our Town* the
playwright acknowledges that he wanted to capture
the reality of this generalized truth.

Three of Wilder's major works won Pulitzer
Prizes: the novel *The Bridge of San Luis Rey* and the
plays *Our Town* and *The Skin of Our Teeth.*

Toward the end of the 'twenties I began to lose pleasure in
going to the theater. I ceased to believe in the stories I saw
presented there. When I did go it was to admire some secondary aspect of the play, the work of a great actor or director or designer. Yet at the same time the conviction was
growing in me that the theater was the greatest of all the
arts. I felt that something had gone wrong with it in my time
and that it was fulfilling only a small part of its potentialities.
I was filled with admiration for presentations of classical

works by Max Reinhardt and Louis Jouvet and the Old Vic, as I was by the best plays of my own time, like [Eugene O'Neill's] *Desire Under the Elms* and [Ben Hecht and Charles MacArthur's] *The Front Page;* but at heart I didn't believe a word of them. I was like a schoolmaster grading a paper; to each of these offerings I gave an A plus, but the condition of mind of one grading a paper is not that of one being overwhelmed by an artistic creation. The response we make when we "believe" a work of the imagination is that of saying: "This is the way things are. I have always known it without being fully aware that I knew it. Now in the presence of this play or novel or poem (or picture or piece of music) I know that I know it." It is this form of knowledge which Plato called "recollection." We have all murdered, in thought; and been murdered. We have all seen the ridiculous in estimable persons and in ourselves. We have all known terror as well as enchantment. Imaginative literature has nothing to say to those who do not recognize—who cannot be *reminded*—of such conditions. Of all the arts the theater is best endowed to awaken this recollection within us—to believe is to say "yes"; but in the theaters of my time I did not feel myself prompted to any such grateful and self-forgetting acquiescence.

This dissatisfaction worried me. I was not ready to condemn myself as blasé and overfastidious, for I knew that I was still capable of belief. I believed every word of [Irish novelist James Joyce's] *Ulysses* and of [French novelist Marcel] Proust and of [German novelist Thomas Mann's] *The Magic Mountain*, as I did of hundreds of plays when I read them. It was on the stage that imaginative narration became false. Finally, my dissatisfaction passed into resentment. I began to feel that the theater was not only inadequate, it was evasive; it did not wish to draw upon its deeper potentialities. I found the word for it: it aimed to be *soothing*. The tragic had no heat; the comic had no bite; the social criticism failed to indict us with responsibility. I began to search for the point where the theater had run off the track, where it had chosen—and been permitted—to become a minor art and an inconsequential diversion.

NINETEENTH-CENTURY THEATRICAL TASTE

The trouble began in the nineteenth century and was connected with the rise of the middle classes—they wanted their theater soothing. There's nothing wrong with the middle classes in themselves. We know that now. The United States and Scandinavia and Germany are middle-class countries, so completely so that they have lost the very memory of their once despised and ludicrous inferiority (they had been inferior not only to the aristocracy but, in human dignity, to the peasantry). When a middle class is new, however, there is much that is wrong with it. When it is emerging from under the shadow of an aristocracy, from the myth and prestige of those well-born Higher-ups, it is alternately insecure and aggressively complacent. It must find its justification and reassurance in making money and displaying it. To this day, members of the middle classes in England, France, and Italy feel themselves to be a little ridiculous and humiliated. The prestige of aristocracies is based upon a dreary untruth, that moral superiority and the qualifications for leadership are transmittable through the chromosomes, and the secondary lie, that the environment afforded by privilege and leisure tends to nurture the flowers of the spirit. An aristocracy, defending and fostering its lie, extracts from the arts only such elements as can further its interests, the aroma and not the sap, the grace and not the trenchancy. Equally harmful to culture is the newly arrived middle class. In the English-speaking world the middle classes came into power early in the nineteenth century and gained control over the theater. They were pious, law-abiding, and industrious. They were assured of eternal life in the next world and, in this, they were squarely seated on Property and the privileges that accompany it. They were attended by devoted servants who knew their place. They were benevolent within certain limits, but chose to ignore wide tracts of injustice and stupidity in the world about them; and they shrank from contemplating those elements within themselves that were ridiculous, shallow, and harmful. They distrusted the passions and tried to deny them. Their questions about the nature of life seemed to be sufficiently answered by the demonstration of financial status and by conformity to some clearly established rules of decorum. These were precarious positions; abysses yawned on either side. The air was loud with questions that must not be asked. These audiences fashioned a theater which could not disturb them. They thronged to melodrama (which deals with tragic possibilities in such a way that you know from the beginning that all will end hap-

138 Readings on Our Town

pily) and to sentimental drama (which accords a total license to the supposition that the wish is father to the
thought) and to comedies in which the characters were so
represented that they always resembled someone else and
not oneself. Between the plays that [English dramatist
Richard] Sheridan wrote in his twenties and the first works
of [Irish-born poet and dramatist Oscar] Wilde and [Irish
dramatist George Bernard] Shaw there was no play of even
moderate interest written in the English language. (Unless
you happen to admire and except Shelley's *The Cenci*.) These
audiences, however, also thronged to Shakespeare. How did
they shield themselves against his probing? How did they
smother the theater—and with such effect that it smothers
us still? The box set was already there, the curtain, the
proscenium, but not taken "seriously"—it was a conve-
nience in view of the weather in northern countries. They
took it seriously and emphasized and enhanced everything
that thus removed, cut off, and boxed the action; they increasingly shut the play up into a museum showcase.

THE NEED FOR DRAMA TO CAPTURE TRUTH

Let us examine why the box-set stage stifles the life in
drama and why and how it militates against belief.

Every action which has ever taken place—every thought,
every emotion—has taken place only once, at one moment
in time and place. "I love you," "I rejoice," "I suffer," have
been said and felt many billions of times, and never twice
the same. Every person who has ever lived has lived an unbroken succession of unique occasions. Yet the more one is
aware of this individuality in experience (innumerable! innumerable!) the more one becomes attentive to what these
disparate moments have in common, to repetitive patterns.
As an artist (or listener or beholder) which "truth" do you
prefer—that of the isolated occasion, or that which includes
and resumes the innumerable? Which truth is more worth
telling? Every age differs in this. Is the Venus de Milo "one
woman"? Is the play *Macbeth* the story of "one destiny"? The
theater is admirably fitted to tell both truths. It has one foot
planted firmly in the particular, since each actor before us
(even when he wears a mask!) is indubitably a living,
breathing "one"; yet it tends and strains to exhibit a general
truth since its relation to a specific "realistic" truth is con-
fused and undermined by the fact that it is an accumulation

of untruths, pretenses, and fiction. The novel is pre-eminently the vehicle of the unique occasion, the theater of the generalized one. It is through the theater's power to raise the exhibited individual action into the realm of idea and type and universal that it is able to evoke our belief. But power is precisely what those nineteenth-century audiences did not—dared not—confront. They tamed it and drew its teeth; squeezed it into that removed showcase. They loaded the stage with specific objects, because every concrete object on the stage fixes and narrows the action to one moment in time and place. (Have you ever noticed that in the plays of Shakespeare no one—except occasionally a ruler—ever sits down? There were not even chairs on the English or Spanish stages in the time of Elizabeth I.) So it was by a jugglery with time that the middle classes devitalized the theater. When you emphasize *place* in the theater, you drag down and limit and harness time to it. You thrust the action back into past time, whereas it is precisely the glory of the stage that it is always "now" there. Under such production methods the characters are all dead before the action starts. You don't have to pay deeply from your heart's participation. No great age in the theater ever attempted to capture the audience's belief through this kind of specification and localization. I became dissatisfied with the theater because I was unable to lend credence to such childish attempts to be "real."

I began writing one-act plays that tried to capture not verisimilitude but reality. In *The Happy Journey to Trenton and Camden* four kitchen chairs represent an automobile and a family travels seventy miles in twenty minutes. Ninety years go by in *The Long Christmas Dinner.* In *Pullman Car Hiawatha* some more plain chairs serve as berths and we hear the very vital statistics of the towns and fields that passengers are traversing; we hear their thoughts; we even hear the planets over their heads. In Chinese drama a character, by straddling a stick, conveys to us that he is on horseback. In almost every No play of the Japanese an actor makes a tour of the stage and we know that he is making a long journey. Think of the ubiquity that Shakespeare's stage afforded for the battle scenes at the close of *Julius Caesar* and *Antony and Cleopatra.* As we see them today what a cutting and hacking of the text takes place—what condescension, what contempt for his dramaturgy.

ABSOLUTE REALITY IN *OUR TOWN*

Our Town is not offered as a picture of life in a New Hampshire village; or as a speculation about the conditions of life after death (that element I merely took from Dante's *Purgatory*). It is an attempt to find a value above all price for the smallest events in our daily life. I have made the claim as preposterous as possible, for I have set the village against the largest dimensions of time and place. The recurrent words in this play (few have noticed it) are "hundreds," "thousands," and "millions." Emily's joys and griefs, her algebra lessons and her birthday presents—what are they when we consider all the billions of girls who have lived, who are living, and who will live? Each individual's assertion to an absolute reality can only be inner, very inner. And here the method of staging finds its justification—in the first two acts there are at least a few chairs and tables; but when Emily revisits the earth and the kitchen to which she descended on her twelfth birthday, the very chairs and table are gone. Our claim, our hope, our despair are in the mind—not in things, not in "scenery." [French dramatist] Molière said that for the theater all he needed was a platform and a passion or two. The climax of this play needs only five square feet of boarding and the passion to know what life means to us.

Our Town as Folk Art

David Castronovo

David Castronovo claims that twentieth-century phenomena such as feminism, complacency, the sexual
revolution, and a fear of conformity prevent a modern
audience from appreciating *Our Town.* As a result, *Our
Town* stands outside the style and content of drama established by playwrights Eugene O'Neill, Tennessee
Williams, and Arthur Miller. Castronovo suggests that
Our Town resembles a traditional folk painting by
memorializing the modest life and simple good works
of Emily and the townspeople of Grover's Corners.

David Castronovo is the author of *Edmund Wilson,*
a book of literary criticism and a contributor of essays to *Collier's Encyclopedia* and *Ungar Encyclopedia of American Literature.*

After seeing a production of *Our Town* in 1969, a young girl
from Harlem commented to a *New York Times* reporter that
she was unable to identify with the characters and situations. Grover's Corners, New Hampshire, was a completely
alien place and its people were in no way relevant to her
concerns. Such a response is not singular or especially un-
sympathetic. From its first tryouts in Princeton prior to the
original New York production in 1938, the play has met with
significant critical and popular resistance. If it isn't the distance of the urban audience from Wilder's small-town setting and values, it is a matter of contemporary sensibility or
fear of sentimentality, or unease about the play's obsession
with mortality, or lack of familiarity with unconventional
theatrical forms. New York audiences did not immediately
take to a play with no scenery and a last act that was set in
a graveyard. Mary McCarthy, writing for *Partisan Review,*
was favorable in her reactions, but somewhat ashamed that
she liked the play. "Could this mean that there was something the matter with me? Was I starting to sell out?" Miss

Excerpted from *Thornton Wilder,* by David Castronovo. Copyright © 1986, by Freder-
ick Ungar Publishing Company. Reprinted by permission of The Continuum Publishing Company.

McCarthy's review was careful to take shots at the scene between Emily and George: "Young love was never so baldly
and tritely gauche" as this. She also made sure that readers
of *Partisan* knew that *Our Town* was "not a play in the accepted sense of the term. It is essentially lyric, not dramatic."
With this comment she was able to set the play apart from
great modern dramas of movement and characterization
like *Six Characters in Search of an Author* or *Miss Julie:* she
could like the play without acknowledging that it was fully a
play. On an emotional level, Eleanor Roosevelt also responded ambivalently—"Yes, *Our Town* was original and interesting. No, it was not an enjoyable evening in the theatre."
She was "moved" and "depressed" beyond words. [American
literary critic] Edmund Wilson's reaction was similarly complicated: Wilder remarks in a letter that Wilson was "so
moved that you found yourself trying to make out a case
against it ever since" (January 31, 1938). Wilson's later pro-
nouncement (letter to Wilder, June 20, 1940) that *Our Town*
was "certainly one of the few first-rate American plays" is far
less revealing about his emotional reaction than the earlier
response. Wilder's play, in short, had its difficulties with
general Broadway audiences, with intellectuals, and with
prominent people of taste and moral sensitivity. For every
[critic] Brooks Atkinson who enthusiastically found "a profound, strange, unworldly significance" in the play, there
was an uncomfortable Mary McCarthy.

Modern Barriers to Appreciating *Our Town*

The barriers that stand between us and *Our Town* are even
more formidable than those of 1938. McCarthy of course
was writing as a literary modern in sympathy with the anti-
Stalinist left: the commitment to experiment of the *Partisan
Review* might have drawn her toward the lyric innovation of
Wilder's work, but behind her reaction was an uneasiness
with Wilder's sentimental situations. Other progressives of
1938, perhaps even Mrs. Roosevelt, were struck by Wilder's
essentially tragic view of human potential: despite what we
aspire to, we are always unaware of life around us and of the
value of our most simple moments. We must face death in
order to see. Such an informing theme could only cause the
liberal, progressive mind to recoil. After more than forty
years, audiences have accumulated attitudes, convictions,
tastes, and experiences that set them farther apart than ever.

Distrust of WASP [white Anglo-Saxon Protestant] America's values, the sexual revolution, feminism, fear of America's complacency, the resistance of many Americans to marriage and family life, the distrust of group mentalities, the rise of ethnic literatures, the general loosening of restraints on language and conduct: such obstacles have wedged their way between us and Wilder's drama. As a scene unfolds—for example, Mrs. Gibbs being gently chastised by her husband for staying out so late at choir practice—the way we live now occupies the stage beside the players, mocking them and pointing up their limitations as fully developed men and women in the modern world.

Many of the roads that lead us to the drama of midcentury seem to be in better shape than the Wilder road: Eugene O'Neill and Tennessee Williams deal with obsession, sexual passion, illness, and torment. Arthur Miller deals with broken American dreams. But Wilder employs the notations of an essentially stable and happy society. To reach his work, we must pay more attention to the situations and themes that he created for people such as ourselves: *Our Town* has our themes, our fears, our confusion; Wilder built the play so that every scene has something to reach us. Our problem has been that whereas other American playwrights have offered encounters with desolation and the tragic isolation of tormented people—the themes of the great modernists and indeed of Wilder himself in his first two novels—Wilder's 1938 play is about another area of our struggle: the essentially ordinary, uncomplicated, yet terrifying battle to realize fully our own ordinary existences. Such a subject obviously is more difficult to present than the more visceral situations that many great contemporary writers have dealt with; but Wilder's style and form are what force the concerns of the play to become familiar truths charged with new vision.

WILDER AS FOLK ARTIST

His style and the design in the play produce the effects of American folk art: in setting, dialogue, and structure, the play comes before the audience like a late-nineteenth-century painting depicting the customs, colors, and destinies of ordinary lives. Whereas O'Neill and Williams give resonance to their characters by exploring hidden motivations and desires, Wilder directs us to the bright surface and the overall pattern of his people's existences. Essentially plotless, the three acts are rooted in theme rather than dramatic movement. We do not so much wait for events or develop curiosity about characters; instead we are made to stand away from the tableau and contemplate three large aspects of earthly existence: daily life, love and marriage, death. As many folk artists do, Wilder positions us at some distance from his subjects: the audience even needs a stage manager to take us into the town and back to 1901. Like the folk artist, Wilder does not care much about verisimilitude, accurate perspective in drawing characters, and shading: "reality" does not require subtlety or many-layered characters or ingenuity of plot. Quoting [French dramatist] Molière, Wilder said that for the theater all he needed "was a platform and a passion or two."

This attitude toward his art can best be understood if we look at Wilder's plot ingredients and observe their affinities to folk art. Act I is packed with natural scenery, social usages, material things, and typical encounters. The sky lightens and the "morning star gets wonderful bright." The town is presented building by building, and then the Gibbses and Webbs are shown in the foreground. Like figures in a typical folk painting, however, the two families are not drawn with careful perspective, and they are no more or no less important than the life that surrounds them in Grover's Corners. They are in the midst of the town and the universe, absorbing and emblemizing social and cosmic concerns. The stage manager dismisses people with, "Thank you, ladies. Thank you very much" just as the folk painter avoids focusing: Wilder's manager switches our attention from Mrs. Gibbs and Mrs. Webb to Professor Willard and his discourse on the natural history of the town. Soon social life and politics are surveyed; the act closes with a cosmic framing of the material. Jane Crofut, Rebecca Webb's friend, received a letter from her minister: after the address the envelope reads—"The United States of America; Continent of North America; Western Hemisphere; The Earth; The Solar System; The Universe; The Mind of God." Rebecca marvels that the postman "brought it just the same." This closing line—with its reminder that the most ordinary address in an average town has a clear relationship to the cosmic order—is Wilder's way of practicing the folk-painter's craft: Grover's Corners lies flat before us, open to the hills and firmament. Every person, object, feeling, and idea takes its place in the tableau of existence. If Wilder had taken the route of probing

Mr. Webb's psyche, he would have ruined the simple design of his composition. Act I, in its multifariousness and plenitude, stands as a kind of celebratory offering to the universe, a playwright's highly colored, two-dimensional rendering of living.

FOLK ART CHARACTERISTICS IN ACT II

Act II is called "Love and Marriage" and takes place in 1904. Once again, it does not appeal to our desire for complex shading and perspective. Character motivation is very simply presented: Emily has always liked George, then has her doubts about him because he is self-centered, and finally feels his capacity for remorse and development. George's motivation for redirecting his life and staying in Grover's Corners after high school is equally direct and simple: "I think that once you've found a person that you're very fond of . . . I mean a person who's fond of you, too, and likes you enough to be interested in your character . . . well, I think that's just as important as college is, and even more so." This is all that Wilder uses to set the act in motion: no ambivalence, no social complications, no disturbances. The primary colors of human love, however, do not preclude the black terror that seizes George before his wedding. He cries out against the pressures and publicness of getting married. Emily's response to the wedding day is no less plaintive; why, she wonders, can't she remain as she is? This apparently awkward doubling of fears and sorrows is the kind of strategy that has made Wilder seem hopelessly out of touch with modern men and women. Indeed, if we are looking for what [Irish poet and dramatist William Butler] Yeats called "the fury and mire of human veins" we have come to the wrong playwright; it is not that Wilder's lovers have no passion. It is simply that their creator has risen above their individuality and sought to measure them against time and the universe. What counts in the historical and cosmic sense is that they are two more accepters of a destiny that connects them with most of humanity: "M . . . marries N . . . millions of them," the stage manager comments at the end of the act. Hardly a romantic, Wilder directs us to the complete unadorned design of the human sequence. "The cottage, the go-cart, the Sunday-afternoon drives in the Ford, the first rheumatism, the grandchildren, the second rheumatism, the deathbed, the reading of the will." There is no mist of feeling, no religious sentiment, no attempt to assign high significance to the procession of events: if audiences find Act II touching—and if some people are moved to tears—the cause is certainly not in any overwriting and pleading for response. Wilder's language is almost bone dry. The stage manager's comments set the mood. As a man who has married two hundred couples, he still has his doubts about one of Grover's Corners' most cherished institutions.

FOLK ART CHARACTERISTICS IN ACT III

Act III is about death and has the form of a memorial folk painting: like many pictures from the nineteenth century that memorialized famous or obscure men and women, Wilder's act brings in scenes from a life—in this case Emily's is featured—and surrounds the central figure with the routines and rituals of ordinary, rather than extraordinary, existence. A typical "important" memorial piece—for instance, the death of George Washington—is filled with references to valor and public deeds; a more modest person's life has the notation of his simple good works. Emily's death, and by extension the deaths of Mrs. Gibbs and lesser characters, is placed in the context of the quotidian. Newly arrived in the graveyard on the hill, the young woman at first refuses to accept her fate and yearns to reexperience the texture of her life. Any day will do; but once she returns to earth on her twelfth birthday, the details of existence—people's voices, a parent's youthful appearance, food and coffee, the gift of a postcard album—are overpowering. Through a clever ironic twist that both prevents the scene from being conventionally sentimental and also forces insight on the audience, Wilder has Emily refusing to mourn or regret. Instead, she throws the burden of loss and blindness on the audience, on the living people who never "realize life while they live it." This very short scene is both birthday and funeral—actually a grim, hard look at the spectacle of human beings, adorned by Wilder with folk motifs: habitual comings and goings, Howie Newsome, the paperboy on his route, breakfast being served. These details have had the curious effect of making some audiences find *Our Town* a cozy vision of New Hampshire life. Looked at in relationship to their structural function—the building up of a dense, ordinary, casual, and unfelt reality to stand against the cosmic order—they are chilling. Like Ivan Ilyich's curtain-hanging (which brings on his fatal illness) or his tickets for the Sarah Bernhardt tragedy (which he can't attend because he is dying), the Wilder folk objects and motifs are frightening fixtures of our lives that once gave pleasure but can only stand in Act III for all the blindness of human existence. After having presented us with this striking fusion of folk art and existential dread, Wilder regrettably mars the last scene with hokum about stars and human aspirations. While this does complete the pattern in Act I where the "Wonderful bright morning star" opens the first scene, it also insists on a kind of message that the experience of the play does not support: only the earth, among the planets and stars, "is straining away, straining away all the time to make something of itself."

This kind of didacticism is disconsonant with and unworthy of Wilder's most fully realized scenes. The fact is that Grover's Corners hardly strains for anything: it isn't very progressive or cultured or enlightened or interesting. Culturally, there is *Robinson Crusoe*, the Bible, Handel's *Largo*, and Whistler's Mother—"those are just about as far as we go." Mrs. Gibbs has cooked thousands of meals. George aspires no higher than—perhaps not as high as—his father. "Straining" to be civilized and to make oneself into something is singularly absent from the play's action. Wilder has instead built up something far less sententious in his three acts: rather than give us yet another American story of social aspiration and the love of democratic vistas, he has used American ordinariness to embody the ardors and terrors of human existence. Tolstoy said of his existential protagonist Ivan Ilyich, "Ivan's life was most simple and most ordinary and therefore most terrible." Wilder would only add "wonderful" in summing up his own characters' lives.

The Charm of
Our Town

Winfield Townley Scott

Winfield Townley Scott maintains that the tone of
Our Town is understatement. Colloquial talk, unheroic characters, casual observations, and dry wit
contribute to this tone. This simple approach convinces the audience of the play's truth and ultimately
assumes a quiet beauty. Despite its soothing nature,
however, *Our Town* does not evade trouble and
tragedy. According to Scott, Wilder's purpose was to
dramatize life, including problems like death, drunkenness, and bawdiness. But Wilder avoids focusing
on the mean and seamy side of life to keep his portrayal of average people balanced and to adhere to
his simple purpose.

   Winfield Townley Scott was a poet and literary
critic. She was the literary editor of the *Providence
(R.I.) Journal.*

As *Our Town* literally begins, Wilder sets in motion the little
wheel of daily doings. This is the only wheel there is in most
plays and fictions; it turns upon the events presented. So here,
it spins with normal activities, the comings and goings and
the conversations, weaving a special era and place and a particular people (though by the way I think Mrs. Gibbs and Mrs.
Webb should not be stringing beans in early May in New
Hampshire); and on through a gentle afternoon to the great
moonlighted night of that May 7 and the ladies strolling chat-
tering home from choir practice.

   This is the realism of the play and, superficially at least, it
is very good. That is, these folk may not be deeply imagined
but they are typically imagined; it is as types of Americana
that they and their Grover's Corners interest us and touch
us. They and the town are unremarkable: we are told so and

we see that it is so; and this of course is the point. The youngsters with their twenty-five cents spending money and love of strawberry phosphates and their school-day affairs, the fathers absorbed in jobs and bringing up these young, the wives similarly absorbed though perhaps a little wistfully aware of larger worlds and startled at just this era that an old highboy might fetch $350 as an antique; yes, we are convinced that this must have been the way it was, and in most essentials still is fifty years later, in that kind of American town. For what the little wheel does in carrying these doings of realism is to give one a sense of changelessness from day to day, year to year: mothers and fathers waken early, they rouse children to breakfast and school, a Joe Crowell, Jr., dependably arrives twice a week with the *Sentinel* and a Howie Newsome every morning with the milk; there is talk of weather which does change season to season but the changes are regular and assured. Far later in the play the Stage Manager remarks something we have known from the first, and known with an intimate feeling, and are not surprised as he said we would be—"on the whole, things don't change much at Grover's Corners."

WILDER'S MANIPULATION OF TIME

Thus this little wheel gives us a sense of timeliness and also, oddly, of timelessness. We are transported back to May 7, 1901. At the same time we sense a certain universality about it; or we sense its *being* as a seemingly permanent thing. And this achievement is the one for which so much writing strives. Nevertheless, we are quickly aware of another dimension which begins to operate when Dr. Gibbs comes on.

We have learned a little earlier that though this is May 7, 1901, in Grover's Corners, New Hampshire, and though the townsman who appears to us as the Stage Manager is there presenting us with this scene and time, he is also existing in our time. He describes stores, streets, schools, churches in the present tense (and this forwards the feeling of changelessness within change as the newly discovered context is revealed), but he suddenly says, "First automobile's going to come along in about five years—belonged to Banker Cartwright, our richest citizen . . . lives in the big white house up on the hill." That remark, which occurs within the first minute or two of the play, strikes the tuningfork: within that sentence the verbs are future, past, present, used with a most guileless insouciance for ordinary discourse. And presently: "There's Doc Gibbs comin' down Main Street now . . . Doc Gibbs died in 1930. The new hospital's named after him. Mrs. Gibbs died first—long time ago in fact. She went out to visit her daughter, Rebecca, who married an insurance man in Canton, Ohio, and died there—pneumonia . . ." and so on. "In our town we like to know the facts about everybody," he sums up matter-of-factly; and then: "That's Doc Gibbs." And Dr. Gibbs gets into a little gab with Joe Crowell, Jr., just as Mrs. Gibbs is seen entering her kitchen to start breakfast.

THE TONE OF *OUR TOWN*

The whole tone of *Our Town* is understatement. The colloquial run of the talk, its occasional dry wit, the unheroic folk, all contribute to this tone. So does the important admission that this *is* a play: we are not bid to suspend our disbelief in the usual way; and so does the bareboard, undecorated presentation. All is simple, modest, easy, plain. And so, in tone, the Stage Manager's revelation is utterly casual. But with it Wilder sets in countermotion to the little wheel a big wheel; and as the little one spins the little doings, the big one begins slowly—slowly—for it is time itself, weighted with birth and marriage and death, with aging and with change. This is the great thing that *Our Town* accomplishes; simultaneously we are made aware of what is momentary and what is eternal. We are involved by the Stage Manager in these presented actions and yet like him we are also apart; we are doubly spectators, having a double vision. We are not asked, as in the presentation of some philosophical concept, to perceive an abstract intellectualism. This is a play—this is art. So we are involved sensually and emotionally. Out of shirt-sleeved methods that would seem to defy all magic, and because of them not in spite of them, Wilder's play soon throttles us with its pathos; convinces and moves us so that we cannot imagine its being done in any other way; assumes a radiant beauty. And indeed we are not taken out of ourselves, we are driven deeper into ourselves. This, we say, is life: apparently monotonous, interminable, safe; really all mutable, brief, and in danger. "My," sighs the dead Mrs. Soames in Act III, "wasn't life awful—and wonderful." For what Wilder's art has reminded us is that beauty is recognizable because of change and life is meaningful because of death.

Later in Act I the Stage Manager deliberately and directly accounts for several future happenings. And again he sums up: "So, friends, this is the way we were in our growing up and in our marrying and in our doctoring and in our living and in our dying." This is the simplest way—and Thornton Wilder can be artfully simple—of saying what *Our Town* is about. It suggests why he chose a spare, documentary style as appropriate to a purpose which can only be termed archeological. But the poetry, so to speak, comes from the juxtaposition of the points of view, human and superhuman, which combine, of course, to a fourth dimension.

The combination admits stars and people, universe and small town, eternity and time, the sense of wonder and the commonplace. This is the music of the play. By the end of Act I its harmonies and its dissonances are interweaving with authoritative power. It beats with the great silence of the moonlight on the streets and gardens of Grover's Corners, on the ladies dispersing from choir practice, on the heliotrope as the doctor and Mrs. Gibbs walk in the yard before retiring, on the weaving progress of drunken Simon Stimson and on Mr. Webb chatting with Constable Warren making his rounds. "Blessed be the tie that binds" is the hymn which, like the ring of the moon, encircles this people. Finally, wistful diminuendo and frank statement of the interwoven tones modulate the conversation of the Gibbs children in the upper window when Rebecca describes the address on a letter Jane Crofut got.

"It said: Jane Crofut; The Crofut Farm; Grover's Corners; Sutton County; New Hampshire; United States of America . . . Continent of North America; Western Hemisphere; the Earth; the Solar System; the Universe; the Mind of God . . . — and the postman brought it just the same!"

"What do you know!" George exclaims.

LITERARY REFERENCES IN *OUR TOWN*

Thornton Wilder is often a literary writer in the derivative sense; it is his severest limitation and makes some of his work pallid and fussy, too much derived from other books. This blight is not upon *Our Town*. Resemblances are momentary. For instance, here is a passage from the much earlier book by James Joyce, *The Portrait of the Artist as a Young Man:*

> He turned to the flyleaf of the geography and read what he had written there: himself, his name and where he was.

Stephen Dedalus
Class of Elements
Conglowes Wood College
Sallins
County Kildare
Ireland
Europe
The World
The Universe

That was in his writing: and Fleming one night for a cod had
written on the opposite page:

Stephen Dedalus is my name,
Ireland is my nation.
Conglowes is my dwellingplace
And heaven my destination.

John V. Kelleher, a Joyce scholar who has kindly done my
research in this matter, adds that the passage is parodied in
Finnegans Wake in one of Isobel's footnotes to the study
chapter: "2. Kellywick, Longfellow's Lodgings, House of
Comments III, Cake Walk, Amusing Avenue, Salt Hill, Co.
Mahogany, Izalond, Terra Firma."

Mr. Kelleher says: "My hunch is that Wilder's use of the
series is taken from Joyce—and why not, after all? Joyce is
only using a couple of standard scrawls that I've often
turned up on the flyleaves of secondhand books, especially
in Ireland." The hunch may be further fortified by Wilder's
avowed use of *Finnegans Wake* in his later play, *The Skin of
Our Teeth*, and by the title of the delightful novel he published just before *Our Town—Heaven's My Destination*. Still,
the title page of *Heaven's My Destination* gives an American
Midwest version of the little rhyme and the address on Jane
Crofut's letter, if it was suggested by the Joyce passage, may
also independently arise from folksay older than memory.
Such material is free to repeated poaching—and indeed all
this is no great matter except for the fun of comparison.

Where *Our Town* reminds one of other writers, also it is
no matter whether with deliberate or accidental echoes, for
the integration is perfect and the resemblances are in every
instance consistent with the regional genre. Here are two or
three:

In the final Act when Emily cries out with love that she
cannot look hard enough at everything, one thinks of the
rather less restrained poem by Edna St. Vincent Millay beginning "O world, I cannot hold thee close enough!" Or, a

little earlier, when the Stage Manager is describing the Grover's Corners cemetery and says, "Yes, an awful lot of sorrow has sort of quieted down up here," one may recall Emily Dickinson's magnificent

> After a hundred years
> Nobody knows the place.
> Agony that enacted there,
> Motionless as peace.

Closer still is yet another New England poem, "To Earth-ward," when the Stage Manager in Act II speaks of the diffi-culty of remembering what it's like to be young. "For some reason," he says, "it is very hard . . . those days when even the little things in life would be almost too exciting to bear. And particularly the days when you were first in love . . ." and so on. The pertinent lines by Robert Frost are:

> Love at the lips was touch
> As sweet as I could bear;
> And once that seemed too much; . . .
> I craved strong sweets, but those
> Seemed strong when I was young;
> The petal of the rose
> It was that stung . . .

FOLK FEELING IN *OUR TOWN*

The resemblances are probably inadvertent. They are pleas-ant evidence of how a particular landscape will sound similar notes in the various minds expressing it. *Our Town* has in fact the quality of folk tale. The "folksiness" of husbands' and wives' conversation, of school kids' talk together, is in tune with the Stage Manager and his wry, affectionate exposition.

"Why sure," says George to Emily as their high school ro-mance dawns on them both. "Why sure, I always thought about you as one of the chief people I thought about." And George's offer to leave his "gold watch" with druggist Morgan as guarantee of payment for the strawberry ice-cream sodas he has recklessly bought Emily and himself bears the same adolescent, awkward sweetness. One thinks of [American novelist and playwright] Booth Tarkington just as one may think, a little later when George and Emily are to be married, of the adolescent-parental relationship in Eugene O'Neill's *Ah! Wilderness.* Dr. Gibbs exclaims, "I tell you, Mrs. G., there's nothing so terrifying in the world as a son. The relation of a father to a son is the damnedest, awkwardest . . . I always come away feeling like a soggy sponge of hypocrisy." But neither Tarkington in his general preoccupation with youth, nor O'Neill in that thin, singular comedy come anywhere near the poetic power, to which the folk feeling is a vital part, of *Our Town.*

The wit is Yankee laconic; sometimes so wry you may ask if it is wit. Noting that lights are on in the distant farmhouses while most of Grover's Corners itself is still dark at six o'clock in the morning, the Stage Manager says, "But town people sleep late." It is funny—but is it funny to the Stage Manager? We have no way of knowing that the Stage Manager does not feel that people who don't get up till six-thirty or seven are late sleepers. This is a part of the charm.

The charm does not evade the big and the ephemeral troubles of life, the tears of youth and of age, and the terminal fact of death. As *Our Town* develops, it is more and more incandescent with the charges of change and of ending. There is not in it any of the ugliness present in the small-town books I have likened it to: the violence and murder in [Mark Twain's] *Tom Sawyer,* the meannesses and frustrations in [Edgar Lee Masters'] *Spoon River Anthology* and [Sherwood Anderson's] *Winesburg, Ohio.* Yet these books also glow with a nostalgic beauty. True, the drunken, disappointed organist would be at home either in Masters' Spoon River or in Robinson's Tilbury Town; and in Act II, at the time of George's wedding, there is the bawdiness of the baseball players which, significantly, the Stage Manager quickly hushes. Brief touches: not much. Nevertheless, I would defend *Our Town* against the instant, obvious question whether Wilder in excluding harsher facts indigenous to life has written a sentimental play, by insisting Wilder would have warped the shape of his plan by such introductions. He was out not to compose a complete small-town history nor, on the other hand, to expose a seamy-sided one; his evident purpose was to dramatize the common essentials of the lives of average people. There are other colors, no doubt more passionate, but they would have deranged this simple purpose which, as I see it, is valid and has been well served.

Deficiencies in
Our Town

John V. Hagopian and Arvin R. Wells

John V. Hagopian and Arvin R. Wells criticize Our Town for being a disguised sentimental comedy. The authors draw the conclusion that the play avoids addressing the depth and complexity of human experience for a conveniently optimistic, middle-class philosophy. Their criticism focuses on three fundamental deficiencies. First, the playwright gives way to a sentimentality that works, at all costs, to have the commonplace aspect of life convey a congenial sensibility. The play's philosophy is evasive, shying away from decisive human insight and resorting to bland sociological generalizations. Second, the authors suggest that Wilder, in his desire to present the universal in everyday normality, passes over opportunities for genuine drama. Finally, characterization in Our Town falls short because the playwright does not probe the psychological interiors of his characters. Hagopian and Wells believe that Wilder sacrifices his drama looking for a stability in American life that does not exist.

John V. Hagopian is a professor of American studies at the University of Saarlandes, Germany. Arvin R. Wells is a professor of English at Ohio University.

Our Town is not in any traditional sense a drama at all; it has neither plot nor conflict, neither complication nor climax. By its abandonment of setting and by its use of the Stage Manager as intermediary between the play and its audience, it gives the appearance of belonging to the experimental theater movement; yet, within the experimental theater it is a completely anomalous production. For all its show of technical virtuosity, it aims at a familiar dramatic effect, that of sentimental comedy which is characterized by its attempt to

Reprinted from John V. Hagopian and Arvin R. Wells, "*Our Town*," in *Insight I: Analyses of American Literature*, edited by John V. Hagopian and Martin Dolch (Frankfurt, Germany: Hirschgraben, 1971) by permission of Arvin R. Wells.

play upon a muted but varied scale of emotions, mingling pathos, nostalgia and humor in a pleasantly innocuous cordial. The popularity of Wilder's play is not difficult to understand when one considers that sentimental comedy continues to dominate the Broadway theater in America and that, from its inception in the 18th century, sentimental comedy has always been popular with a large middle-class audience. Its popularity derives from the fact that it has, at bottom, the effect of complimenting us upon the lives that we lead by assuring us that the surface patterns of our lives are life itself and that, though we do not always appreciate it, ordinary life is, after all, good. It treats life with genteel laughter and death with appropriate tears and, despite a frequent show of profundity, takes neither very seriously.

However, because it disposes of the necessity of a coherently developed story line, *Our Town* avoids immediate identification with this familiar dramatic category. In itself, it is perhaps best described as a recitation in character of a quasi-philosophical essay, illustrated by selected vignettes from small-town life. The subheadings which the Stage Manager gives the three acts of the play—Daily Life; Love and Marriage; Death—put one in mind of books of popular sociology and philosophy; and the Stage Manager is, himself, a traditional character often known as a "cracker barrel philosopher" or "rural sage." Moreover, the absence of a proscenium curtain and the reduction of setting to a few properties serves to eliminate the normal expectations of a theater audience and to keep complete control in the hands of the Stage Manager, who lectures the audience and arranges brief dramatic sketches for its amusement and edification. Revolutionary as it may seem at first glance, however, *Our Town* is not quite a reduction to what [French dramatist] Molière cited as the minimum essentials of drama—a platform and a passion or two. As [American drama critic] George Jean Nathan has pointed out, Mr. Wilder cheats in the use he makes of skeletonized drama:

> While insisting that he abandons all scenery and props, he still compromises with his plan by employing them. He shows us no houses, but he brings out two flower-covered latticed doorways to trick the imagination into an acceptance of their presence . . . He uses almost as many lighting tricks as the late Belasco [for] sunsets, dawns, and sunrises. He asks us to . . . picture a garden or pasture or chicken patch and then pulls a vaudeville act by having someone in the wings moo

like a cow or crow like a rooster. He concretely shows us no marriage altar, but he puts his little actress into a white bridal costume and then has the electrician throw a stereopticon slide of a stained-glass window above the spot where he has asked us to visualize it.

THE STAGE MANAGER

Nevertheless, the play is not the thing; what matters is the discourse. True to the tradition of the rural sage, the Stage Manager invites the audience to contemplate the superficial patterns of small-town life through the warm glow of his shrewd but benevolent personality. He has no coherently thought out point of view but unself-consciously mixes sentimentalized naturalism with a kind of ambiguous supernaturalism. He is, in fact, not a thinker at all; he is an observer with a certain understanding of the value of the sort of facts that the "rural savant" and Editor Webb are called in to provide, facts which suggest that his way of seeing things is rooted in a concrete awareness of the immensity of time and nature as well as of the here and now. Because he deals with the big, general experiences of mankind—love, marriage, death—what he says carries a gratuitous hint of profundity; yet, he avoids pompousness by a studied pose of simplicity and matter-of-factness, which is a form of anti-intellectualism, and by his gift for detached statements informed by a shrewd, practical wit.

In effect, the Stage Manager attempts to lead the audience to assent to the proposition that the minimal existence of Grover's Corners is an adequate base for encompassing the experiences and finding out the fate of mankind. If the audience takes him seriously, it must accept the assumption that what matters most in human existence is apparent in the limited world which the Stage Manager does, in fact, present. And if this is accepted, the audience may miss the fact that the amused condescension, the shrewdness and the matter-of-factness of the Stage Manager disguise the sentimentality of his viewpoint—"sentimentality" here meaning an unwarrantedly high valuation in moral, emotional and aesthetic terms of the thing presented.

Such sentimentality is the inevitable product of any attempt to make the most commonplace surfaces of life carry the burden of a congenial but amorphous "philosophy," and its presence in Wilder's play is particularly obvious when the play is placed in the context of the rest of 20th century

American literature. In these terms, *Our Town* reads as a competently executed but nonetheless sentimental response to the widespread attack upon the stifling ethos and cultural poverty of American small-town life (cf. Sinclair Lewis's *Main Street*). It responds by shifting the focus from those who rebel against the poverty of such a life to those who, superficially regarded, appear contented with it and whose lives remain safely within the middle range of emotion and awareness. Even Wilder's own view of the play supports such a reading:

> *Our Town* is not offered as a picture of life in a New Hampshire village; or as a speculation about the conditions of life after death (that element I merely took from Dante's *Purgatory*). It is an attempt to find a value beyond all price for the smallest events in our daily life. I have made the claim as preposterous as possible, for I have set the village against the largest dimensions of time and place.

These dimensions are referred to most emphatically at the end of act I when Rebecca Gibbs tells her brother about the elaborately addressed letter Jane Crofut received from the minister of her church:

> . . . Grover's Corners . . . the United States of America; Continent of North America; Western Hemisphere; the Earth; the Solar System; the Universe; the Mind of God.

PHILOSOPHICAL EVASIVENESS IN *OUR TOWN*

Though the comments of the Stage Manager imply that through these tepid, unexamined lives we are looking at the core of human experience, no human experience is, as a matter of fact, looked at other than obliquely: birth is a light burning across the tracks; love is finding out that the girl or boy next door has been watching you, and death is a few black umbrellas and tears and a dignified immobility. Whatever hard-fact details he includes are not those of elemental human experience, but of sociology; *Our Town* might well serve as an excellent source of information concerning small-town life in New England before World War I.

Even the "daring" device of the third act, the commentary of the dead, will not bear close examination. Despite the philosophical flourish with which it is introduced—"Everybody knows that there is something eternal"—the play at this point becomes more than usually evasive. The line between life and death is deliberately blurred: the grief and the fearful sense of finality that dwells on this side of the line is evaded, and the profound mystery—even if only the mystery of nothingness—that dwells on the other side is reduced to the non-committal terms of forgetting and waiting. Death, so conceived, provides a viewpoint from which the still living may not be too harshly criticized for failing to look with perpetual, wide-eyed wonder upon the familiar conditions of their daily lives. Actually, this somewhat elaborate device seems designed simply to gain an uncritical assent to Emily's "Oh, earth, you're too wonderful for anybody to realize you," which comes as close as any statement in the play to expressing the theme.

Our Town as Non-Drama

Wilder comes closer than any other modern dramatist to writing non-drama, and he does so deliberately. The maximum of stock response is elicited from the minimum of dramatic action. As Editor Webb says, "Very ordinary town, if you ask me. Little better behaved than most. Probably a lot duller." When Wilder attempts to present the universal in this statistically normal particular, he cannot help citing and then deliberately pushing off-stage potential sources of genuine drama. For example, in the very first dialogue of the play, the paper-boy seeing Doc Gibbs returning from a night-call asks, "Somebody been sick, Doc?" "No," says Doc Gibbs, "Just some twins born over in Polish town." In the total context of the play, this has the same effect as [Mark Twain's] Huck Finn's answer to Aunt Sally's question on hearing of an explosion on a steamboat, "Was anybody hurt?" "No. Just a nigger killed." In this smug, middle-class, Anglo-Saxon small town the Goruslawskis hardly rate as human beings. One would think that in a population of 2,640, the birth of twins, even in a Polish family, warrants just a bit more excitement. To a more significant playwright, the impact of Polish immigrants on the Anglo-Saxon population is material for powerful drama—*vide* Tennessee Williams' *Streetcar Named Desire.* But in this play, the Poles and the Catholic church are safely relegated to the other side of the railroad tracks.

At another point in the play, a man in the audience asks Mr. Webb, publisher and editor of The Grover's Corners *Sentinel,* "Is there no one in town aware of social injustice and industrial inequality?" And the facetious answer is, "Oh yes, everybody is,—somethin' terrible. Seems like they spend

most of their time talking about who's rich and who's poor."
If they do, we hear none of that talk in this play, and out goes
the Ibsen-Miller tradition.

Thornton Wilder, like every artist, is faced with a problem
in the selection of details; and he has chosen to select only
the most ordinary, everyday details of a very small, narrow
segment of the American population—a sort of socio-
philosophical cross-section of the genus homo Americanus,
Anglo-Saxiensis. And he is extra-ordinarily successful in
rendering the ordinary. His most crucial flaw in this respect
is a revealing one: Emily, dying in childbirth becomes quite
an exception to the statistical norm—an exception perfectly
suited to Wilder's sentimental purposes. No doubt *Our Town*
will always have a strong appeal to delicately sensitive adolescents; the mature observer will respond as Arthur Miller
did, suspecting that its popular appeal lies in "the deep longing of the audience for such stability, a stability which in
daylight out on the streets does not exist . . . the play falls
short . . . because it could not plumb the psychological in-
terior lives of its characters and still keep its present form."

Our Town is fairly representative of Wilder's point of view,
his talent and his deficiencies. Because his writings fail to reflect any serious attempt to come to terms with the depth and
complexity of human experience, the overt expression in
them of a congenial and basically optimistic "philosophy"
stands out as an unearned increment. It is for this reason that
Wilder has not gained recognition from American literary
critics and scholars. Standards seem to be different in Germany if Horst Oppel is right in predicting "with complete cer-
tainty that *Our Town* will prove to have had a permanent effect [on playwriting] in Germany." So far there is not much
evidence of that effect, however, as Oppel himself emphasizes
"that among the newer German playwrights there is not a
single one who has successfully followed in Wilder's foot-
steps." Nevertheless, it is one of the most amazing phenomena
of modern literary history that in Germany Wilder continues
to be celebrated as a great world author while in his own
country he is generally regarded as merely an interesting literary curiosity. [The following discussion highlights specific
deficiencies in the staging and characterization of *Our Town*.]

1. *What is the effect of eliminating the proscenium curtain
and the usual stage setting?*

In general, this diminishes the normal "aesthetic distance" between the audience and what is presented on the stage and defeats the audience's usual dramatic expectations. To the extent that the device is successful, it undermines the critical assumptions of the audience and renders critical objectivity more difficult. Moreover, the device serves to keep control in the hands of the Stage Manager, allowing him to dominate the entire play.

2. *How does the Stage Manager function in the play? What is his relationship to the audience? Is his relationship to the characters in the play a constant one?*

The Stage Manager, under the pretense of telling us about Grover's Corners, shapes the play as an expression of his understanding and evaluation of human existence. He is something of an amateur philosopher, and what he presents is not so much a commentary on the play as it is a loosely conceived discourse in which the dramatic scenes serve as illustration. In his relationship to the audience, he functions as an informal lecturer and, thereby, gains the authority implicit in the lecturer's position. His relationship to the characters in the play varies from act to act. In the first act, he assumes the role of neighbor and fellow citizen; in the second, he becomes the spiritual and philosophical voice of the community, and in the third, he assumes some of the lesser attributes of God, conceived in the popular image of a noncommittal but kindly disposed old man.

3. *From what point of view does the Stage Manager evaluate the human experiences presented in the play?*

His basic assumption, which is stated in his speech before the wedding (Act II), is that nature is an essentially benevolent force and that it is in some way striving for the perfection of man. Each individual participates unconsciously in the striving of nature; this makes life, ipso facto, meaningful, and the individual need only keep himself alert, to *look at* people and things, in order to realize the goodness of it. For, while life may not seem to be interesting and meaningful as most people live it, rightly perceived it is full of wonder and a poignant sweetness. In any event, man cannot lose the future because not only is nature on his side but there is *something* eternal in him which will survive. Unfortunately, there is nothing in the play to suggest that the Stage Manager holds these beliefs for any reason other than that they are comfortable and reassuring.

4. *For what purposes are the "rural savant" and Editor*

Webb called upon in Act I? What do the hecklers in the audience contribute?

Prof. Willard and Editor Webb help to establish Grover's Corners as a real place; they do not, however, add anything concrete to our awareness of either the appearance or the atmosphere of this particular town. On the contrary, their citations of facts and statistics simultaneously imply the reality of the town and reduce it to a representative abstraction. This reduction is important in the development of the play, which has to do, after all, not with Grover's Corners but with "Our Town" with the ordinary places in which presumably the majority of men live out their ordinary lives. The Stage Manager might have assumed this function but only at the risk of lessening his rapport with the audience. Introducing the "rural savant" and calling upon Editor Webb spares the Stage Manager both the burden of uncharacteristic pedantry and the necessity of entering into controversy with the hecklers.

The hecklers, themselves, are written in as a kind of controlled audience response. They raise the questions and state the objections that the more critical and sceptical members of the audience might be expected to entertain. Each of the questions represents one of the points of view from which small-town life is frequently attacked. Editor Webb meets each with apparent common sense and humility, and even when he has no direct answer to the implied criticism, his attitude in contrast to the aggressive, uncharitable tones of the hecklers is calculated to win the audience to the defense of the small town. Thus, the hecklers serve to foster the feeling that the usual critique of small-town life is irrelevant, the intellectual plaything of cranks and snobs.

5. *"Our Town" consists of loosely connected dramatic sketches taken from the lives of a few Grover's Corners inhabitants. How, then, does Wilder contrive to give the play continuity?*

There is, of course, the bare hint of a plot in the developing relationship between George Gibbs and Emily Webb. Moreover, though the play spans several years, the fact that it begins at dawn with talk of birth and ends at night with talk of death gives it the appearance of unity and completeness. Most important, however, is the personality and point of view of the Stage Manager. It is immediately established as a convention of the play that the Stage Manager may direct our attention wherever he wishes. He assumes the responsibility for providing transitions, and it is soon understood that the dramatic elements in the play are subordinate to the elaboration of his point of view.

6. *What is the role of Simon Stimson in the play?*

In a sense, he is the devil's advocate. Unlike the other characters he has been hurt and embittered by life, and, consequently, he dissents from the point of view of the Stage Manager. Thus, the play might be said to have both a thesis and an antithesis; however, no real conflict is allowed to develop. For the nature of Simon's hurt is left vague, and he is not allowed a voice until the last act, in the context of which his dissent is made to appear strictly personal and even pitiable.

Chronology

1897

Thornton Niven Wilder is born in Madison, Wisconsin, on April 17. His identical twin dies within a few hours of birth.

1906–1911

Father, Amos P. Wilder, is appointed American consul general to Hong Kong; the family accompanies him to his new post, where Thornton attends a German school. After only six months, Isabella Wilder, Thornton's mother, takes the children to Berkeley, California, where they reside until 1911.

1911

The family rejoins their father in Shanghai, where he is now posted. After a short stint at another German school, Thornton attends the China Inland Mission Boys and Girls School at Chefoo.

1912–1915

Back in California, Thornton attends school in Ojai and Berkeley, graduating from Berkeley High School in 1915.

1914–1918

World War I; the United States enters the war in 1917.

1915–1917

Wilder attends Oberlin College in Ohio; some of his earliest works are published in the *Oberlin Literary Magazine.*

1917

Transfers to Yale University in New Haven, Connecticut.

1918

Yale Literary Magazine publishes several of his short plays and essays.

1918–1919

After a summer working for the War Industries Board in Washington, D.C., tries to enlist, but several armed services reject him for poor eyesight. Accepted by the Coast Artillery Corps, he serves for a few months as a corporal in Rhode Island, after which he returns to Yale.

1920

After serving for a year on the editorial board of the *Yale Literary Magazine* (which publishes his play *The Trumpet Shall Sound* as a serial), he graduates with a bachelor of arts degree. F. Scott Fitzgerald publishes *This Side of Paradise;* Sinclair Lewis publishes *Main Street;* Nineteenth Amendment grants women the right to vote.

1920–1921

In Rome, at the American Academy, Wilder studies archeology and begins writing *The Cabala*. After a year abroad, he returns to the United States to teach French at Lawrenceville, a boys' school in New Jersey.

1922

Fitzgerald publishes *The Beautiful and Damned;* James Joyce publishes *Ulysses;* T.S. Eliot publishes *The Waste Land.*

1924

Takes a leave of absence to attend graduate school at Princeton University.

1925

Receives M.A. in French literature from Princeton; spends the summer at MacDowell Colony in New Hampshire. Begins writing *The Bridge of San Luis Rey*, continuing to work on it in Europe that fall. Fitzgerald publishes *The Great Gatsby.*

1926

The Cabala is published. Ernest Hemingway publishes *The Sun Also Rises.*

1927

Wilder returns to Lawrenceville; *The Bridge of San Luis Rey* is published.

1928

Receives Pulitzer Prize for *The Bridge of San Luis Rey*. Publishes *The Angel That Troubled the Waters*. Resigns from Lawrenceville and goes to Europe, where he works on *The Woman of Andros*.

1929

William Faulkner publishes *The Sound and the Fury*.

1929–1937

Great Depression follows the stock market crash of October 29, 1929.

1930

Wilder publishes *The Woman of Andros*. Begins lecturing in comparative literature at the University of Chicago.

1931

Publishes *The Long Christmas Dinner and Other Plays*.

1933

President Franklin Roosevelt introduces his New Deal, programs intended to end the depression.

1935

Wilder meets Gertrude Stein, beginning a long, warm friendship. Publishes *Heaven's My Destination*. Italy invades Ethiopia.

1936–1939

Spanish Civil War.

1937

Japan invades China.

1938

Germany annexes Austria. *Our Town* opens in New York, receives Pulitzer Prize. *The Merchant of Yonkers* opens in New York.

1939

John Steinbeck publishes *The Grapes of Wrath.*

1939–1945

World War II. The United States enters the war in 1941, after the December 7 Japanese attack on Pearl Harbor.

1942

Wilder writes movie script *The Shadow of a Doubt* for Alfred Hitchcock. Enlists in the air force, where he is commissioned a captain. *The Skin of Our Teeth* opens in New York.

1942–1943

Serves in Africa. Receives his third Pulitzer Prize in 1943 for *The Skin of Our Teeth.*

1945

Leaves the air force in September.

1948

Publishes *The Ides of March.*

1950–1951

Awarded the Charles Eliot Norton Professorship of Poetry at Harvard University, where he lectures on "The American Characteristics in Classic American Literature."

1952

American Academy of Arts and Letters awards him its gold medal for fiction.

1963

Awarded the Presidential Medal of Freedom.

1964

Hello, Dolly!, based on *The Matchmaker,* first produced for the stage.

1965

Awarded the National Medal of Literature.

1967

Publishes *The Eighth Day.*

1968

Awarded the National Book Award for *The Eighth Day.*

1973

Publishes *Theophilus North.*

1975

Thornton Wilder dies December 7.

FOR FURTHER RESEARCH

WORKS BY THORNTON WILDER

Alcestiad, or A Life in the Sun. *With a Satyr Play*, The Drunken Sisters. New York: Harper and Row, 1977.

"American Characteristics" and Other Essays. Ed. Donald Gallup. New York: Harper and Row, 1997.

The Angel That Troubled the Waters *and Other Plays*. New York: Coward-McCann, 1928.

The Bridge of San Luis Rey. New York: Albert & Charles Boni, 1927.

The Cabala. New York: Albert & Charles Boni, 1926.

The Eighth Day. New York: Harper and Row, 1967.

Heaven's My Destination. New York: Harper & Brothers, 1935.

The Ides of March. New York: Harper & Brothers, 1948.

The Journals of Thornton Wilder, 1939–1961. Ed. Donald Gallup. New Haven, CT: Yale University Press, 1985.

The Long Christmas Dinner *and Other Plays*. New York: Coward-McCann, 1931.

The Merchant of Yonkers. New York: Harper & Brothers, 1939.

Theophilus North. New York: Harper and Row, 1973.

Three Plays: Our Town, The Skin of Our Teeth, The Matchmaker. New York: Harper & Brothers, 1957.

The Woman of Andros. New York: Albert & Charles Boni, 1930.

BIOGRAPHICAL WORKS ABOUT AND INTERVIEWS WITH THORNTON WILDER

E.K. Brown, "A Christian Humanist," *University of Toronto Quarterly*, April 1935.

Jackson R. Bryer, ed., *Conversations with Thornton Wilder*. Jackson: University Press of Mississippi, 1992.

Edward Burns, Ulla E. Dydo, and William Rice, eds., *The Letters of Gertrude Stein and Thornton Wilder*. New Haven, CT: Yale University Press, 1996.

Malcolm Cowley, "The Man Who Abolished Time," *Saturday Review of Literature*, October 6, 1956.

Richard H. Goldstone, *Thornton Wilder: An Intimate Portrait*. New York: E.P. Dutton, 1975.

Tyrone Guthrie, *A Life in the Theatre*. New York: McGraw-Hill, 1959.

———, "The World of Thornton Wilder," *New York Times Magazine*, November 27, 1955.

Gilbert A. Harrison, *The Enthusiast: A Life of Thornton Wilder*. New York: Ticknor & Fields, 1983.

Linda Simon, *Thornton Wilder: His World*. Garden City, NY: Doubleday, 1979.

Robert van Gelder, "Interview with a Best-Selling Author: Thornton Wilder," *Cosmopolitan*, April 1948.

Amos Niven Wilder, *Thornton Wilder and His Public*. Philadelphia: Fortress Press, 1980.

ABOUT *OUR TOWN* AND WILDER'S PLAYS

Martin Blank, ed., *Critical Essays on Thornton Wilder*. New York: G.K. Hall, 1996.

Rex Burband, *Thornton Wilder*. Twayne's United States Authors Series 5. New Haven, CT: College and University Press, 1961.

Malcolm Cowley, introduction to *A Thornton Wilder Trio*. New York: Criterion Books, 1956.

Richard Gilman, *The Making of Modern Drama*. New York: Farrar, Straus, and Giroux, 1974.

Richard H. Goldstone and Gary Anderson, *Thornton Wilder: An Annotated Bibliography of Works by and About Thornton Wilder*. New York: AMS Press, 1982.

Bernard Grebanier, *Thornton Wilder*. Minneapolis: University of Minnesota Press, 1964.

Paul Lifton, *Vast Encyclopedia: The Theatre of Thornton Wilder*. Westport, CT: Greenwood Press, 1995.

Elizabeth Barron McCasland, *The Philosophy of Thornton Wilder*. New York: Carlton Press, 1976.

Glenway Wescott, *Images of Truth*. New York: Harper and Row, 1962.

There are a variety of Wilder resources on the Internet. The editors direct interested readers to a website being developed by the Columbia University Graduate School of the Arts, in honor of Wilder's centenary, as a promising starting point for research. Find the website at www.columbia.edu/cu/arts/ wilder/index.html. Its "wilder.net" link on the Education Resources page claims it will link to "every on-line resource with a connection to Thornton Wilder."

INDEX